ENVIRONMENTAL DESIGN SOURCEBOOK

Published by RIBA Publishing, 66 Portland Place, London, W1B 1AD

ISBN 9781859469606

British Library Cataloguing-in-Publication Data
A catalogue record for this book is available from the British Library.

Commissioning Editor: Alex White
Assistant Editor: Clare Holloway
Production: Jane Rogers
Designed and typeset by Alex Synge
Cover design: Alex Synge
Printed and bound by L.E.G.O S.p.A Italy

www.ribapublishing.com

INNOVATIVE IDEAS FOR A SUSTAINABLE BUILT ENVIRONMENT

ENVIRONMENTAL DESIGN SOURCEBOOK

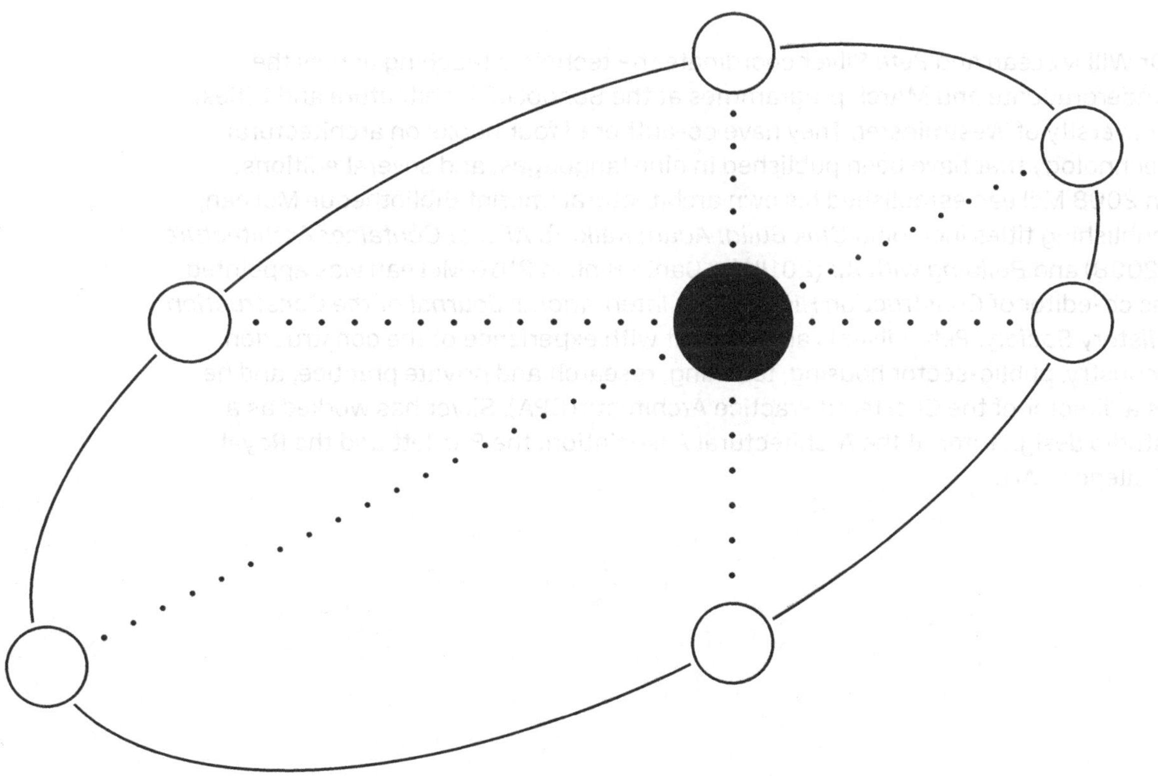

RIBA Publishing

Will McLean and Pete Silver

Acknowledgements

The authors would like to thank the many generous contributors who have supplied information and images that make up this book. We would like to particularly thank John Hutchinson (Ecos Maclean) and Paul Bavister (Flanagan Lawrence/UCL) for their unique and valuable authored contributions, and John Farrell (XCO2) for his excellent information on thermal comfort. We would also like to thank colleagues Scott Batty, Rosa Schiano-Phan and longtime collaborator Chris Leung (UCL). We would also like to extend a special thank you to former student and recent University of Westminster MArch graduate Urangua Sodnomjamts for her fascinating research and photography of the Mongolian *ger*. This book is dedicated to the memory of Simon Veglio (1959–2021).

About the Authors

Dr Will McLean and Pete Silver coordinate the technical teaching across the undergraduate and MArch programmes at the School of Architecture and Cities, University of Westminster. They have co-authored four books on architectural technology that have been published in nine languages, and several editions. In 2008 McLean established his own architectural imprint Bibliotheque McLean, publishing titles including *Quik Build: Adam Kalkin's ABC of Container Architecture* (2008) and *Building with Air* (2014) by Dante Bini. In 2016 McLean was appointed as co-editor of *Construction History: The International Journal of the Construction History Society.* Pete Silver is an architect with experience of the construction industry, public-sector housing, teaching, research and private practice, and he is a director of the Chartered Practice Architects (CPA). Silver has worked as a studio design tutor at the Architectural Association, the Bartlett and the Royal College of Art.

Contents

‘Nature is neither good nor evil. Only we and our products can be good or evil.’[1]

Frei Otto

Introduction

In May 2019, the UK Parliament declared 'a national climate emergency', and the United Nations has said that we might only have until 2030 to limit a climate change catastrophe. In June 2019, student group Architects Declare issued 'Open Letter to the Architectural Community: A Call for Curriculum Change':

'Ecology should not be an afterthought; it must be elevated and wholly integrated into all aspects of the curriculum, and serve as one of the primary tenets through which we understand our roles as responsible members of the Earth's ecological community.' – Architects Declare, 2019

To date, there might have been a sense that creating an ecological, or sustainable, architecture was a choice – and that so-called 'green' environmental design and technological solutions could appear rudimentary, unexciting and worthy. Currently, an increasingly informed and engaged student body is both exercised and energised by the problem of design in the age of climate change. A new social and ecological prerogative demands appropriate material choices, a reinvention of construction, and evolving building programmes that look at life cycle, embodied energy, energy use and relative sustainability.

Sustainable design requires a multivalent approach to the use and understanding of environmental design technology, and does not take a singular imperative as a starting point. Biomimetics, fluid dynamics, evaporative cooling, deployability and biofabricated material construction are all included, as are bio-remediation, solar geometry and thermal labyrinths. This book is an attempt to capture a contemporary philosophy of environmentally informed technology, and introduce students and professionals to the current and future trends in the development of an ecologically sustainable architecture.

We want students to learn from the fabric formwork of Dante Bini and the radically different earth-building techniques of Stéphanie Chaltiel and Rowland Keable, and be inspired by the dynamic bi-metallic building skin of Doris Sung, which moves and shades with the heat of the sun. If we believe in the anti-entropic potential of design, of 'doing more with less', then we need to make visible (and explicable) the huge palette of design and technological strategies, solutions, products and inventions that are available to students and designers.

We aim to inspire and inform students about a wide range of sustainable design and technological strategies and approaches. The book will introduce students to key concepts in relation to the embodied energy of construction, material properties, the environmental performance of buildings, and how to 'passively' control building climate for human comfort and minimise energy consumption. Further, it aims to demystify 'environmental design' as a purely technical exercise, and encourage students to understand the principles by which we heat, cool, moderate, mitigate and remediate our environment. The challenge of climate change is the challenge of all good design, where resources, efficiency, ingenuity and appropriateness should be explored in equal measure and to best effect. The theme and contents are globally relevant, but the specific application of these strategies and technologies is necessarily local and specific (differing climate conditions, construction materials, etc.).

Given the recent government declaration of a climate emergency, the book presents a survey of available technologies and design strategies for the ecological designers and architects of the future. It is intended to provide useful references, practical information and simple explanations for environmental design ideas. Designers need to be inspired by new and ancient approaches to environmental design in the useful mediation and moderation of climate, which architecture can afford. Environmental design includes knowledge about climate, materials, engineering, construction and energy (embodied and in-use), as well as building performance, and these are covered as a broad overview of the subject. Where possible, we have included numerical data about the relative performance of designs and materials. Many of the projects do not have performance indicators as such, but their inclusion is important for inspiration and provocation. Architecture cannot learn from architecture alone, and the necessary eclecticism of this book is informed by nature, science, industry and the arts.

'The construction sector accounts for approximately 50% by weight of all material taken from the Earth's crust, and 40% of the world's energy consumption is required to operate buildings. The building industry is depleting natural resources beyond sustainable levels. At the time of writing and by some estimates, the production and transportation of building materials alone constitutes some 45% of all CO_2 used in the construction process and around 70% of a building's total life cycle carbon (its carbon footprint) is emitted before it is even occupied.'[2]
–United Nations Environment Programme, 2017

The intention of this sourcebook is to set out a palette of possibilities for the sustainable design of the built environment, i.e. in consideration of the responsible use of natural resources. Architects, engineers and builders have always been mindful of how they use natural resources, largely in order to control building costs, which in turn created a need for technical innovation and efficiency. At the same time, traditional structures are not necessarily less environmentally efficient than contemporary ones: buildings were born out of the local environment – both making use of its physical resources and reacting to its climate. Whether from trees, rocks, mud or snow, each material has found a way to be employed as both structural form and climatic envelope. The responsible use of natural resources in the built environment may be assessed in terms of both its *embodied energy* – the efficient use of construction materials and the efficiency of the construction process, and its *operational energy* – the environmental efficiency of the completed building, particularly as a climatic enclosure.

The efficient use of construction materials begins with the sourcing of the raw materials. The only renewable materials are organic, and therefore these are the most sustainable. For example, as of 2022, all new public buildings financed by the French state must contain 50% wood or other organic material. With inorganic materials, their responsible use depends on how much of the resource is known to be available. Stone and clay are still found in abundance, but even sand – that is *sharp* sand used for building (which, along with gravel, represents the highest volume of building material used on earth after water) – is running out.[3]

The second consideration with respect to raw materials is the efficiency of their extraction or harvesting: how much and indeed what type of energy is used in these processes. This book does not specifically address renewable energy supply, but we should recognise the rapidly changing energy supply mix in the UK, the recent success of large-scale offshore wind supply, and the (if yet undecided) future technologies of carbon capture and storage, hydrogen, tidal barrage schemes and so on. And of course, where the materials are being sourced from, and how much energy is required to transport them to factories for processing or to the construction site. Much of the Victorian London housing stock was built from the clay on which the city stands and fired locally in small kilns. How might we usefully employ new digital technology to fabricate locally?

The need for processing raw materials into building materials is the next phase to consider (for example, turning iron ore into steel or limestone into cement – both very high-energy processes). Often these processes do take place at source, such as at logging mills and stone quarries, but many construction components (including large-scale elements, up to and including entire dwellings) pass through a number of specialist (pre)fabrication processes before arriving on site. Richard Buckminster Fuller was arguing as far back as the mid-1960s that there was little need (with some rare exceptions) for further mining of metal ores when there was more iron and bauxite out of the ground (in the form of steel and aluminium) than there was in the ground.[4] Metals are easily recycled with minimal material wastage, and the electric arc furnaces used are much more energy-efficient than blast furnaces used to smelt mined ore into metals.

Once on site, what will be the lifespan of the building: of the raw materials, components and elements from which it is constructed? Is the carbon footprint of the construction of a building that has been designed to last 1,000 years ten times less than one that will last 100? Or can the building's materials be successfully upcycled, recycled or repurposed? The design of the built environment plays a major role in the responsible use of construction materials. Choices made by the designer will determine the type and quantity of materials used, and great savings can be made through structural efficiency. The relative weight of building components affects the size and weight of the building structure and its unseen foundations.

The efficiency of the construction process begins with design: the choice of structural and enclosure systems will determine this process. Large-scale prefabrication (including contemporary digital manufacturing techniques) might be appropriate – fabricators optimise their use of materials with 'nesting' software to minimise wastage in sheet stock such as glass, metals and timber. It might also be useful to apply vernacular solutions. What resources – workforce, expertise, manufacturing and industrial processes – are locally available? There is a history of innovative solutions to old problems, of traditional solutions to new problems, and of technology transfer from other industries, all of which can aid low-energy (low-carbon) construction.

The environmental efficiency of completed buildings is chiefly with respect to their performance as climatic envelopes. This will vary according to the climatic zone of the site and the availability of appropriate resources (see above). In principle, the variables that built environment designers can control consist of both *passive* and *active* measures, including reactive (or responsive) elements. Passive elements include the fabric of the building (use of thermal mass, insulation, glazing and shading systems), natural ventilation for both air exchange and cooling, and orientation with respect to the sun and wind.

As a designer working in an age of recognisable climate change, it would be nonsensical not to both respond and rise to the challenge of creating transformative and sustainable design. The complex environmental, social and economic context for students is sizeable, but should not overawe the clear-thinking designer who can navigate the technical and programmatic imperatives of a design project. This is not a rulebook or manual, but a sourcebook of ideas, technologies and approaches for inspiration and reflection. The shift in emphasis of sustainability to encompass both energy (in use) and the embodied energy of what buildings are actually made from, how they are engineered and constructed offers an exciting opportunity for the designer to define environmental design.

‘Health should be at the forefront of the architecture curriculum, as the driver for sustainable design.’[5]

Beth Bennett-Britton

Chapter 1
Climate and Human Comfort

The environmental factors that provide the necessary conditions for human comfort and survival are quite specific, and define a narrow set of upper and lower temperature and humidity levels. Humankind's imperative, by choice or otherwise, to live across the globe in a range of climatically challenging locales, in pursuit of food and work, is proof of both human ingenuity and local adaptation. The environmental designer and campaigner John-Paul Frazer used to give a talk for undergraduate students entitled 'Learning from the Locals',[6] in which he described the insects, animals and plants that could survive in extreme heat or coolth. Frazer would explain the processes by which a beetle might condense water on its wings in a waterless desert, or a prairie dog would regulate the temperature of its complex network of burrows through careful siting (elevation and orientation). Frazer's point was that we should study local adaptation in nature, and that if we extend that study to include local (vernacular) architecture we would build a greater understanding of how to work with our local environment to achieve human comfort through dynamic and symbiotic design and construction. The relatively new branch of engineering known as *biomimetics* provides design solutions that are inspired by, but do not copy, nature.

The following chapter outlines key areas of environmental design science that begin with the operational details of human comfort. It describes conditions *critical* for human survival as well as conditions *desirable* for human comfort, for which the designer should strive. Solar geometry is explained in simple diagrammatic terms, but is common to all technologies and designs featured throughout this book. All our energy comes directly or indirectly from the sun. Wind and acoustics are discussed as environmental factors that we can harness, mitigate and tune for our comfort and pleasure, as are thermal mass and insulation, which we can employ to regulate the temperature of our buildings. Harold Hay, who is quoted in this chapter, undertook fascinating research into dynamic thermal mass and insulation, and how we might change and deploy these properties as required. It is important that designers continue to question the assumptions and received wisdom of construction knowledge and building performance.

The climate zones as defined by the Köppen–Geiger map help to classify climatic regions and can provide designers with a 'rule of thumb' for passive design measures, but we must remember that climate is dynamic and now more than ever is subject to change. The psychrometric chart graphically situates an ideal temperature and humidity for our basic comfort, but interestingly this 'comfort envelope' can be extended with simple passive measures such as local shade or breeze, and this less hermetic and more dynamic view of thermal comfort has the potential to reduce both the *embodied energy* and *energy in use* of architecture. Computational fluid dynamic (CFD) software was until recently the domain of the engineering specialist, but with its relative ubiquity and likewise the augmented reality of solar geometry phone apps, we now have at our fingertips powerful analytical 'design' tools that we should usefully employ.

→ **Fig 1.02.5** Diagram showing relative scale (but not distance) relationship between the sun and the earth (in blue). The diameter of earth at the equator is 12,756 kilometres and the diameter of the sun is 1,392,700 kilometres (over 109 times larger).

1.01	**Human Comfort**

'Alliesthesia helps explain certain aspects of comfort under transient conditions, like the anticipatory effect on sensation and comfort following moving from one set of thermal conditions to another.'[7]

–Asit Mishra, et al.

Human comfort is chiefly dependent on thermal comfort and maintaining the body at an acceptable temperature. Through the process of thermoregulation, our core body temperature remains at a relatively constant 36.5–37.5°C. When we are too hot we lose heat mainly through the evaporation of sweat (perspiration), but when humidity levels are very high (above 80%) evaporation rates drop and our ability to cool ourselves is radically reduced. For human comfort, relative humidity should be between 40 and 70%. When we are too cold our bodies start to shiver, which increases body heat and we also get 'goose bumps', created when muscles at the base of each body hair contract and pull the hair upright, trapping air next to the skin to create a layer of thermal insulation. As humans have lost most of their body hair, the reflex is now largely obsolete and we depend on clothing or buildings to maintain our comfort. We can locally mitigate the effects of heat with simple measures such as a breeze from a window or fan; local air movement of 0.5 metres per second can provide an equivalent temperature reduction of around 3°C.

Alliesthesia describes a kind of thermal pleasure derived from ideas of adaptive comfort in buildings, which might afford pleasant thermal changes or differentiation throughout a building related to specific functional requirements such as sleeping or eating. Local lighting levels can also be a personal and subjective issue. It is not advisable for designers to apply generic standards to the provision of servicing in buildings, as this has a financial and environmental cost and does not necessarily support or enhance human comfort. Professor Andy Ford stated that 'the relationship between numbers and human comfort has to be made meaningful, or it will be seen as boring',[8] which is a valuable provocation to urge designers to verify numeric data against personal experience and judgement.

Other environmental factors key to maintaining and improving conditions critical for human comfort are:

- good air quality, and ensuring the supply of clean air within enclosed spaces
- illumination, and the provision of adequate daylighting and light levels
- good acoustics, for clarity of communication and protection from unwanted noise pollution from neighbouring rooms, buildings and the wider environment
- sanitation, for clean water supply and waste disposal.

There is an increasing focus on the provenance of construction materials and their relative toxicity in relation to the 'off-gassing' of volatile organic compounds (VOCs) contained in synthetic materials and finishes, which can be obviated or eliminated through the use of environmentally benign alternatives.

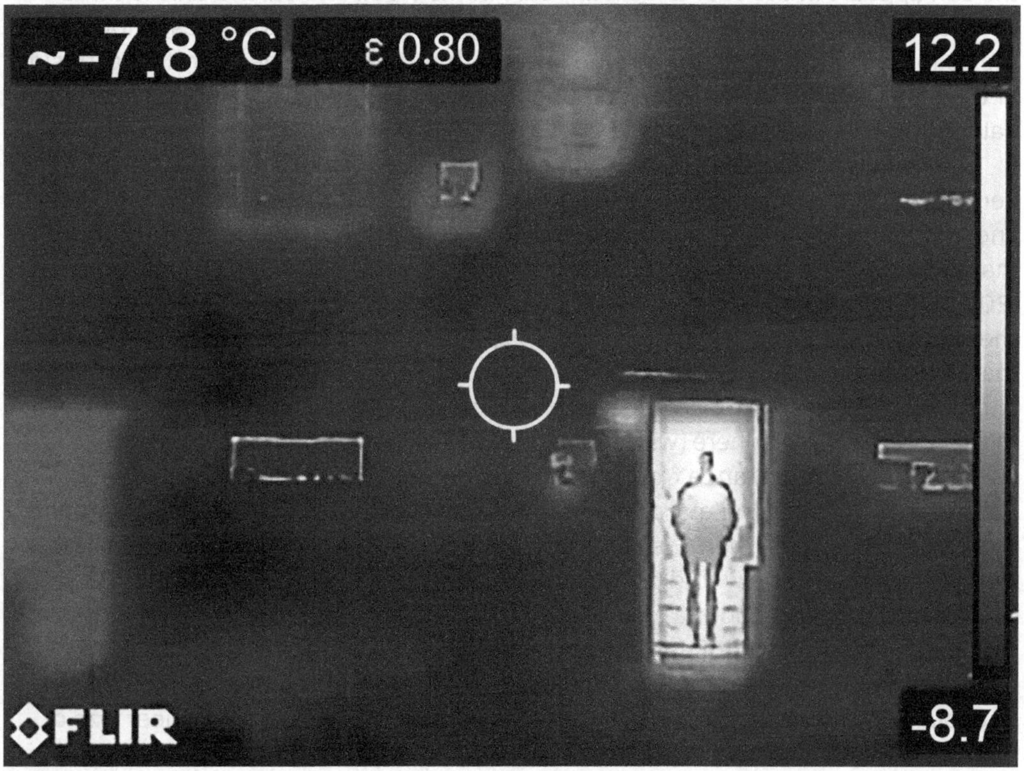

↑ **Fig 1.01.1** A thermal image or thermogram captures the long-infrared frequencies of the electromagnetic spectrum, so can visualise temperature. This increasingly ubiquitous technology (used to diagnose Covid-19 at airports) can be used to accurately measure human temperature as well as the relative thermal insulative performance of building fabric – or how much heat a wall traps or emits.

1.02 Solar Geometry

'A well-conceived and constructed building will interact positively with the local climate during its entire lifetime, thus minimizing its dependency on non-renewable resources.'[9]

– Livia Tirone

The earth orbits the sun in an anticlockwise elliptical orbit once every 365.26 days. It spins anticlockwise on its north–south axis once every day, which explains why the sun appears in the east and disappears in the west. The earth's axis is tilted with respect to the plane of its orbit at an angle of about 23.4 degrees, known as the ecliptic. This tilt (or ecliptic plane) means that for half of the year the north side of the earth is tilted towards the sun and the south is tilted away and, for the other half of the year, the reverse is true.

The equatorial plane divides the earth into the northern and southern hemispheres. The intersection of the equatorial and ecliptic planes is called the line of equinoxes. At two points in the earth's orbit this line intersects the sun, marking (in the northern hemisphere) the start of spring (20 March) or autumn (20 September). Perpendicular to the line of equinoxes is a line which contains the solstices, and when the northern hemisphere is most tilted towards the sun, it marks the longest day of the year (summer solstice, June 21) while the southern hemisphere has its winter solstice, and vice versa with the shortest day of the year in the northern hemisphere (winter solstice, 21 December).

The average distance from the earth to the sun is around 150 million kilometres (93 million miles), and writer H.G. Wells explains their relative distance and dimensions: '... If, then, we represent our earth as a little ball of one inch [24.5 mm] diameter, the sun would be a big globe nine feet [2.74 m] across and 323 yards [295 m] away, that is about a fifth of a mile [a third of a km], four or five minutes' walking'.[10] The diameter of earth at the equator is 12,756 kilometres and the diameter of the sun is 1,392,700 kilometres (over 109 times larger), which helps to explain why sunlight can be described as parallel rays, due to the sheer size of the sun in relation to the earth. When experimenting with small physical design models, it is worth remembering that the light of a desk lamp is not collimated (or parallel), so if the sky is clear (and you can determine which way is north) then it is always advisable to test sun-path modelling and shadow-casting in the open air. As Buckminster Fuller exclaimed, 'The most important thing to teach your children is that the sun does not rise and set. It is the Earth that revolves around the sun'.[11]

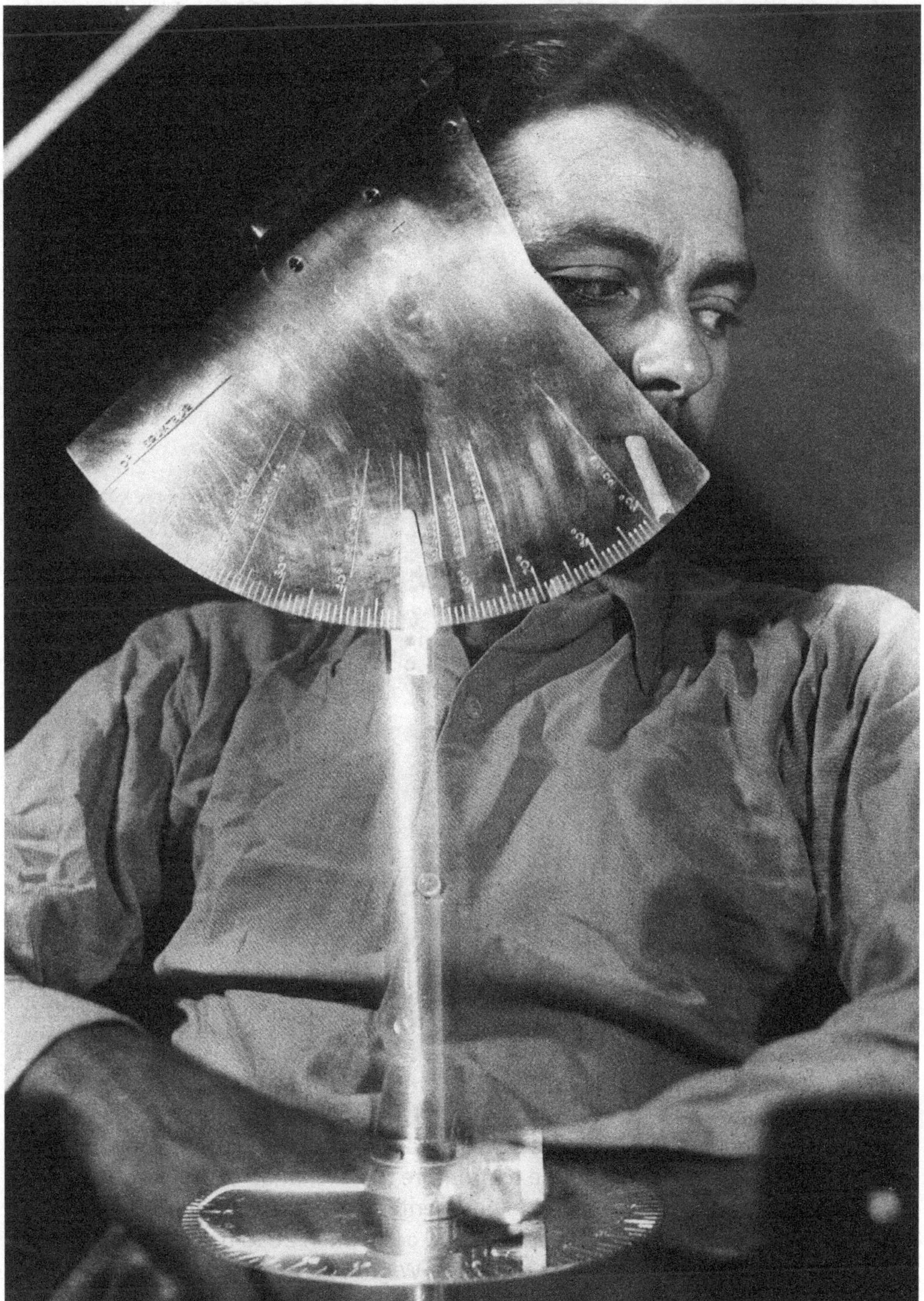

↑ **Fig 1.02.1** Ernő Goldfinger posing with a solar inclinometer for measuring sun angles.

← **Fig 1.02.2** Three 'blinkered mirror' solar structures with guest critic Ted Cullinan. Studio in the Woods workshop, Isle of Wight, 2010.

↓ **Fig 1.02.3** Detail of mirror structures designed to reflect the sun at a particular time of day and year. Studio in the Woods workshop, Isle of Wight, 2010.

Architects Gianni Botsford and Kate Darby established Studio in the Woods as an ongoing educational programme to promote the exchange of architectural knowledge and skills through direct experimentation. These workshops have specifically researched issues of sunlight and context. In 2010 the Studio in the Woods workshop took place on the Isle of Wight and explored the relative movement of the sun with a series of 1:1 static 'blinkered mirror' structures, designed to reflect the sun at a given time. A film of the interaction of sun and mirrors brilliantly reveals the dynamic (and fast-moving) relationship between sun and earth.

Some of the earliest and best-known structures built across the world were designed to reveal the solar geometries and relationships of solstice, season and time. The Great Temple at Abu Simbel, Egypt is designed on a specific axis to let light enter the temple on 22 October and 22 February, whereas the Temple at Karnak, Egypt appears to be aligned to celebrate the midwinter solstice. The stone circles of Stonehenge, Wiltshire and Ceann Hulaveg, Callanish, Isle of Lewis are both widely believed to be aligned with respect to the winter and summer solstices, and to celebrate midsummer and midwinter sunrise and sunset.

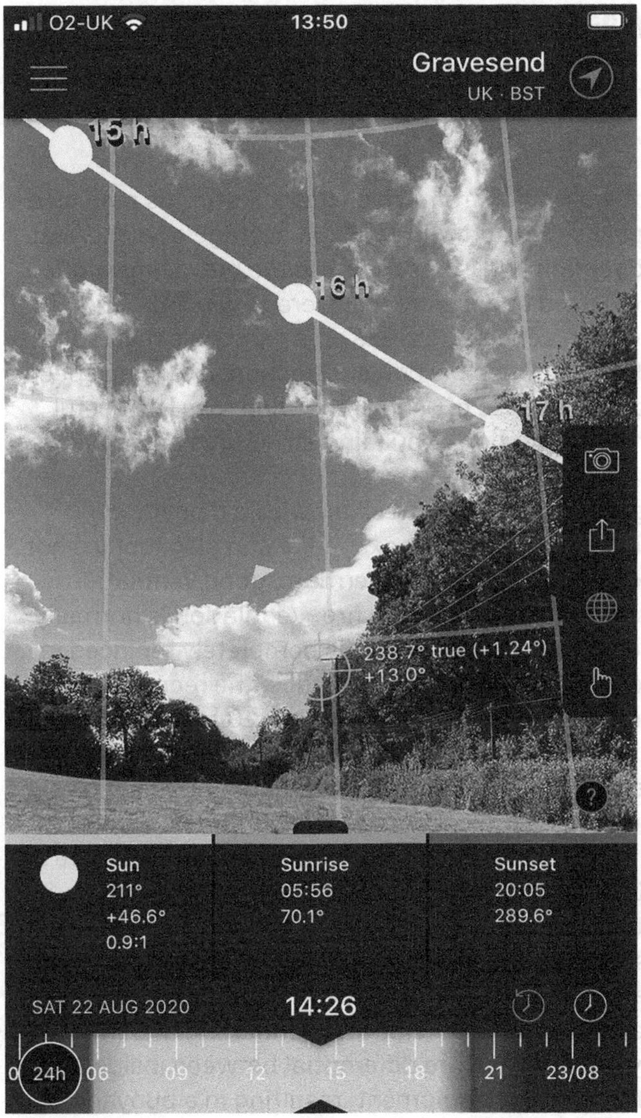

↑ **Fig 1.02.4** Phone apps such as SunSurveyor provide excellent site-specific and real-time sun angle information.

1.03 Wind, Air Movement and Ventilation

'Heating and cooling account for a significant proportion of energy use in buildings (e.g. 50% in the USA).[12] These high energy costs could be reduced by using ventilation strategies that make use of naturally occurring wind and buoyancy forces to drive flows.'[13]

–Dr Megan Davies Wykes

Wind is described in relation to the direction from which it originates, as read on a compass. For any given geographical location, wind will, on average over the year, tend to come from a particular direction and is described as the *prevailing wind.* A wind rose is a graphical notation used to describe the average wind direction and wind speed for any location. Each concentric circle on a wind rose represents the percentage of time the wind blows from a particular direction, and wind speed measured in m/s is also denoted with the use of colour. The wind rose is a useful design tool to establish the correct orientation of building structures and make use of natural air movement.

Ventilation is the exchange of stale air with fresh air within a building, replacing carbon dioxide and supplying oxygen. Air exchange can also replace hot air with cool air and moderate relative humidity. Furthermore, good ventilation is essential for the evacuation of smoke in the event of a fire. Ventilation is normally measured by the number of times that the air in a room is completely replaced in an hour, described as air changes per hour (ac/h). For an office, the recommended rate is between 4 and 6 ac/h, and for a restaurant it is between 10 and 15 ac/h. In order to mitigate the energy used in the ventilation of buildings and avoid the use of air-conditioning systems we should naturally ventilate our buildings where possible. Buildings can be designed to encourage and control natural air movement using a number of simple strategies such as cross-ventilation. There are two main types of natural ventilation: wind-driven and buoyancy-driven. Cross-ventilation occurs in rooms that have window openings on opposite sides of a room – wind hitting a building can result in a high pressure on the windward side and a converse low pressure at the leeward side, and this pressure differential can create an internal flow, bringing fresh air in from the outside and ventilating a room. Ventilation can also be driven by the temperature differential between inside and outside. Incoming air is heated by people or equipment, resulting in a buoyancy-driven flow at a window, but this does depend on the position of that window, as the hot (buoyant) air wants to escape at the top of a room, drawing in cooler air at the base. Buoyancy-driven ventilation systems that use vertical building elements such as chimneys, vents and stairwells can be said to employ the 'stack effect'.

In the wind-catcher towers of Iran (see page 128) a sophisticated combination of these technologies provides both cooling and ventilation.

CFD models (see page 26) are increasingly being used to study the complex three-dimensional flows of air in and around a building – using the shape and surface morphology of the architecture to drive air movement and ventilation.

↑ **Fig 1.03.1** The Lanchester Library, Coventry University is the largest naturally ventilated deep-plan building in Europe. The 50 m square-plan library floors are ventilated via a series of five lightwells that double as air delivery shafts. The chimney-like structures draw out the stale air. Alan Short and Associates, developed with Brian Ford, 2000.

→ Fig 1.03.2 A rotating timber cowl integrated into the roof of an old granary building in Kent. These structures are more typically seen atop the oasthouses of Kent and Sussex, designed to dry hops. The rotating cowl keeps the open (ventilated) side of the chimney in the leeward side of the wind.

1.04	**Acoustics: Noise, Sound, Music and Architecture**
	Designer/Researcher Paul Bavister (Flanagan Lawrence/UCL)

'Wherever we are, what we hear is mostly noise. When we ignore it, it disturbs us. When we listen to it, we find it fascinating.'[14]

– John Cage

The perception of electromagnetic radiation through highly developed sensors in the back of an ocular sensor is one of the fundamental methods that most species on the planet use to understand their environment – determining shape, colour and distance using reflected light. For most humans this is undoubtedly our primary sense, and our other senses are unconsciously relegated to a position of (perceived) lesser importance. Hearing is generally considered useful for conversation and music, and for a vague sense of 'ambient awareness'. The sounds our ears pick up are just as complex as light, but our minds subconsciously process the data, so we really are not aware of what our ears are telling us most of the time. We are listening out for a few core signals, and otherwise we are happy to consciously ignore our audial sense. In this way, listening is analogous to riding a bike; we are aware we are doing it but unaware of how we are doing it, and what it is telling us. Yet, if we were to remove just a few acoustic input signals, we would suddenly notice a sharp drop in awareness. A few moments spent in an anechoic chamber highlights this. The lack of spatial sound cues, room reflections and reverberation robs us of spatial acuity, leaving us marooned in formless space, with an overpowering feeling of helplessness and isolation. For many this is a deeply uncomfortable experience, and most people cannot spend more than 30 minutes in such a space.

Sound is a fundamental part of our existence, and because we generally ignore it, some sounds are annoying. This annoyance can lead to a sense of discomfort, and if prolonged, a lowering of wellbeing. Noise has been acknowledged as a cause of health problems, leading to regulatory change in the building codes. These steps help mitigate problems such as noise pollution, but they don't go far enough. Sound is a fundamental part of the WELL Building Standard™,[15] yet there are currently no clear metrics in use to determine a path forward. What is the role of the architect in this position? Is playing birdsong and white noise into offices really an effective way of dealing with such problems? Are there more creative alternatives?

Research being undertaken at UCL's Bartlett School of Architecture on psychophysiological responses to sound and space via electrodermal activity (skin conductance) and heart-rate analysis is showing us a new world of the body's response to sound, and new methods of modulating how we feel in different spaces with different sounds. This is giving us a new palette of tools with which to engage with sound and the body in space in a much more creative way.

↑ **Fig 1.04.1** According to recent World Health Organization (WHO) findings, noise is the second largest environmental cause of health problems after the impact of air pollution. Disguised urban noise monitoring experiment by Will McLean.

→→ **Fig 1.04.2** The Denge 'sound mirrors' were constructed on the Kent coast in the 1920s as early-warning devices to hear approaching aircraft. They became obsolete with the invention of radar, but their parabolic forms – which collect and concentrate sound to a point (listener or microphone) are a great visual analogue of how designers can collect, reflect and focus sound.

1.05 Designing for Different Climatic Zones

'... much can be done for comfort cooling in a house by proper architectural design and selection of materials.'[16]

– Farrington Daniels

Knowledge of climatic conditions such as temperature, humidity, wind direction and intensity, rain, and solar geometry and intensity can ensure that human comfort levels are maintained throughout the year with the careful tailoring of passive design principles in response to the local environment. One of the most widely used climate classification systems is the Köppen–Geiger map. This was originally published by Wladimir Peter Köppen in 1884 and was latterly developed by Rudolf Geiger, and has become widely known as the Köppen–Geiger climate classification system. Köppen–Geiger classifies climate into five main classes (A–E) and 30 sub-types, with their classification based on air temperature, precipitation and vegetation:

- A – tropical
- B – dry
- C – temperate
- D – continental
- E – polar

Based on these key climate types and the requirements for maintaining human comfort within buildings, key passive design measures can be employed for the successful mitigation and management of local climate. The following short overview is based on work by environmental designer John Farrell.

Hot and humid (tropical) zones

Solar shading can be used to reduce solar gains, with shallow horizontal shades on north and south facades (blocking 40–60° solar angles) and shutters or vertical shades for east and west facades. The use of lightweight structures to minimise thermal mass allows buildings to cool more quickly. Light-coloured, well-insulated roofs with ventilated roofspaces minimise solar heat gains. Good ventilation is critical, with cross-ventilation utilising local winds, which can be improved by minimising east and west facades with long, narrow building forms.

Hot and dry zones

Solar shading can be used to reduce solar gains, with shallow horizontal shades for east and west facades (blocking 50–70° solar angles) and shutters or vertical shades for east and west facades. Light-coloured, well-insulated roofs with ventilated roofspaces minimise solar heat gains. Exposed thermal mass can utilise diurnal temperature variation through thermal lag to moderate internal temperatures. Ventilation rates can be kept low during the day and increased overnight to purge excess heat energy. Evaporation and transpiration cooling features such as shallow water pools and vegetation can be employed. A compact building form will reduce surface area to minimize heat gain, with internal courtyards used for shade and ventilation.

Temperate zones
Solar shading can be used to reduce solar gains in the summer (blocking 55–70° solar angles), but lower winter sun allowed into the building can be used in conjunction with thermal mass to provide ambient heat. Deep horizontal shading or roof overhangs can be used on facades pointing towards the equator, with vertical shades or shutters on east and west facades. Thermally massive building construction can utilise the diurnal temperature range to regulate internal building temperature. A thermally well-insulated building fabric will minimise heat loss in winter and heat gains during the summer. Deciduous planting can be used to provide seasonal shading.

Cool zones
In cool zones, provide windbreaks against prevailing winter winds, and minimise window openings or opening size on the windward side. Allow winter sun to reach equator-facing windows to provide passive thermal heat. High levels of thermal insulation are critical, while allowing for sufficient internal ventilation.

As with all architecture, the orientation and siting of the building is critical for good environmental control and mitigation, and the conflicting criteria of a 'view' versus solar gain or 'view' versus building shelter and shade should be carefully considered.

↑ **Fig 1.05.1** Deciduous plants can be used to provide solar shade and transpiration cooling in the summer and allow sunlight and thermal gain in the winter.

1.06 The Climatic Envelope

'We paint the collectors of our solar energy systems black and our barn and factory roofs white ... black does not always absorb the sun's rays and white does not always reflect it in just the way we've been taught to believe. There's also what I call "cool black" and "warm white".'[17]

– Harold Hay

Harold Hay was interested in why the Bedouin tribes of North Africa wore large thick black headscarves and their tents were dark in colour, in seeming opposition to the widely understood logic of heat absorption and reflectance. Hay explains that if Bedouin tents were white some sunlight would be reflected into the tent, making it brighter but also hotter. The Bedouin tent isn't cooler inside than outside – but, as importantly, it isn't hotter. Likewise, the whiteness of a polar bear allows solar energy to be '... reflected from hair to hair downward until it reaches the skin where it converts to heat under the insulation and helps warm the body'.[18]

Buildings can be designed to control their internal environments both actively and passively. Active environmental control typically involves using energy to power fans, air-conditioning, heating systems and active shading systems in order to maintain a satisfactory level of thermal comfort. A passive climatic envelope uses the form and fabric of the building to maximise the benefits of ambient energy flows from the natural environment, with the building envelope controlling heat gain, heat loss, ventilation and natural light. In temperate climates, new (and well-insulated) buildings tend to produce a level of heat from their occupants and equipment such as lighting, computers and so on to the extent that they are likely to need cooling rather than heating. The World Health Organization defines temperatures of between 18 and 24°C as being a healthy range for indoor environments, with maximum acceptable temperatures between 25 and 32°C. This presents quite a range, and it can be shown that it is possible to extend the 'comfort envelope' of acceptable temperature levels with additional physiological measures such as increased air flow, protection from direct sunlight and material specification.

↑ **Fig 1.06.1** Second Dome is an air-supported structure designed by the Spanish architecture practice DOSIS for creative workspace provider Second Home. London Fields, 2016.

→ **Fig 1.06.2** Second Dome by DOSIS is supported by continuous air pressure from a series of small portable fan units.

Architects use the terms *climatic envelope, building envelope* and *building skin* to refer to the layer (or layers) of building fabric that soak up or reflect the heat, light, wind and sound to control/moderate internal climate and human comfort. The climatic envelope or skin should be the most dynamic component of a building, and should passively respond with diurnal and seasonal change to create conditions conducive to different kinds of desirable living, working and recreational environments. An increased interest in the interstitial spaces of winter gardens, conservatories and lobby spaces presents the designer with a new palette of differentiated climate to support human needs and desires, and not a uniformity of internal environment.

1.07 Thermal Mass

'It's a very low-technology idea that almost anyone can understand and use and it works.'[19]

–Steve Baer

Thermal mass is the ability of a material to absorb, store and release heat energy. It requires a considerable amount of heat energy to change the temperature of high-density materials such as concrete, rammed earth, brick or stone. These high-density, heavyweight materials can therefore be said to have high thermal mass. Lightweight (less dense) materials, such as timber, have low thermal mass and cannot store heat in the same way. Thermal mass can be usefully employed as a design measure in buildings to help to capture, store and release heat energy as required. It can act as a 'thermal battery', helping to regulate internal building temperature. In a winter condition with low sun angles, if we allow the sun to shine on a heavyweight floor or internal wall, that surface will slowly absorb heat throughout the day and subsequently release it at night, helping to maintain an even temperature. Similarly, the thick stone wall of a Mediterranean house will protect the house from daytime heat, with the heat energy absorbed throughout the day and released at night-time. The time that the heat energy takes to travel through the thermal mass of stone is described as 'thermal lag'.

Projects such as Harold Hay's Roofpond (see page 126) and Steve Baer's Zome House (see page 122) utilise the excellent thermal capacity of water as the thermal mass, which can be added after the construction of the house. In a trombe wall, the heat absorption of a thermally massive wall is increased with the addition of an insulated glazed layer in front of the (sun-facing) wall. Sunlight passes through the glazing, and when this short-wavelength radiation hits the dark surface of the thermal mass, energy is absorbed and re-emitted in the form of longer-wavelength radiation that cannot pass back through the glazing. This is known as the 'greenhouse effect', and it explains how the wall stores heat for later release into the building.

When building for a hot and humid climate, lightweight construction is used to shield inhabitants from the sun, while maximising ventilation up through and across the structure. A building like this is trying very hard not to store any heat energy at all.

↑ Fig 1.07.1 Thermally massive internal atrium walls in a highly insulated timber building help to regulate the building temperature during the day. Rivergreen Development Offices built by Rammed Earth Consulting.

1.08 Thermal Insulation

'If we take enough time and effort to design something properly (currently an expensive occupation), it needs half the amount of material and can still be more durable.'[20]

– Professor Julian F.V. Vincent

Thermal insulation is used in buildings to provide a barrier to the flow of heat energy and keep buildings warm or cool. According to local climate, it is important to establish whether insulation is required to keep the heat in or out, or both. Heat energy is transmitted by conduction, convection or radiation. Conduction is the transfer of energy through matter from atom to atom. For example, a metal spoon placed in a cup of hot tea becomes warmer because the heat from the liquid is conducted along the spoon – metals are good thermal conductors. Convection is the transfer of heat energy in a gas or liquid by movement of currents: we can see heat leaving the hot teacup as rising steam. Radiation is the direct transfer of energy through electromagnetic waves – most importantly, the sunlight that heats our planet. Materials with a high thermal mass are not usually good thermal insulators because they have good thermal conductivity. Good thermal insulation depends on the ability of a material to resist heat passing through it. Such materials are said to have poor thermal conductivity.

The most common types of thermal insulation resist the transfer of conducted and convected heat by relying on pockets of trapped air within their structure. Typically their thermal resistance works regardless of the direction of heat flow. Recent developments in embedding phase-change materials (PCMs, see page 46) within thermal insulation can create a more thermally dynamic wall that transfers more or less heat through it, depending on internal and external temperature. Natural thermal insulation materials include cellulose fibre (paper or wood pulp), cork (see page 136), straw and sheep's wool.

One of the most common types of thermal insulation is mineral wool made from basalt and steel slag waste, in a process that sees the volcanic rock heated until molten and then spun into fine fibres like candyfloss. This process is energy-intensive, but mineral wool has good fire and water resistance. Expanded foam insulation is also ubiquitous, and there are now non-fossil fuel (plant-oil) based expanding foams that use soy and castor oil.

One of the newest forms and most efficient types of thermal insulation is aerogel, used as both a solid and as an aerogel blanket. Aerogels are among the lightest solid materials in existence, and they were originally made from silica, a mined material. Because aerogel describes a manufacturing process rather than a chemical composition, new cellulose (and thus more environmentally benign) aerogels are currently being developed for the construction industry. The relative

← **Fig 1.08.1** Peter Tsou, a scientist at the Jet Propulsion Lab, holds a block of aerogel. Aerogel is extremely light (it is made of 99% air), and is an excellent thermal insulator.

thermal performance of a given insulation material becomes critical if you are trying to minimise wall thickness, for instance: to achieve a U-value of 0.15 W/m^2K (see below) you might need more than 250 mm of mineral wool, whereas you could achieve the same insulative value with an aerogel blanket of 70 mm, or even a vacuum insulated panel of 20 mm thickness – less than one-tenth of the thickness.

The rate at which heat is conducted through a particular material under specified conditions is described as its thermal conductivity and is measured in watts per metre kelvin (W/mK) and known as its K-value. The thermal resistance of a material is described as the R-value, and is the reciprocal of thermal conductivity, which is dependent on its thickness and can be calculated as $R = t/K$ (where t is the thickness of the material). The ability of a material or 'build-up' of materials in a wall, roof or window to transfer heat energy from one side to the other is thermal transmittance, which is measured per area per temperature difference. The formula is expressed as watts per square metre per degree celsius (W/m^2K), and the resulting figure is known as the U-value. Although standard U-values have been calculated for specific types of walls, any combination of materials may be calculated by adding together their R-values along with values for surface transmittance. So to find the heat loss per square metre, simply divide the temperature difference by the sum of the R-values.

Thermal (cold) bridging is where a thermally conductive material directly connects from the outside to the inside of a building (and vice versa), allowing heat or coolth to pass through it, increasing heat loss and causing potential problems with condensation occurring at these 'bridge' points.

1.09 Computational Fluid Dynamics

'Things hitherto hidden from the human eye could be penetrated and made visible.'[21]

– György Kepes

CFD provides an important visual output for the complex algebra of the Navier–Stokes equations. CFD software allows the engineer and designer to visually model the flows of any 'fluid' medium including water, wind, blood or smoke. The use of such software was pioneered for engineering applications such as improving the aerodynamics of an aeroplane or car, or the hydrodynamics of a boat. If we reverse-engineer this process and the designed object is fixed, as most buildings are, we can usefully employ CFD to better understand the movement of air both inside and around a given building design. We can then use CFD in combination with local weather data (prevailing winds, etc.) to simulate and design natural ventilation and cooling systems for the building. CFD modelling can provide the designer with instant, simulated feedback on the relative performance of naturally wind-driven internal ventilation and cooling strategies. The three-dimensional CFD model of a building can then be tweaked and adjusted with an almost instantaneous iterative design process, helping to improve building performance with the use of visual feedback. CFD modelling is a powerful new design tool, which has migrated from specialist use in the optimisation of high-value engineering such as turbine blades and racing cars, and is now available to the student.

This process of making the invisible visible is mirrored in the graphic output of finite element analysis (FEA), which has enabled structural engineers to better understand structural behaviour by making forces visible. Increased knowledge of structural behaviour can help to optimise structural performance and reduce material usage and thus mitigate embodied energy. The mathematics of CFD is not only scalable and non-specific in its viscous medium, but it also produces an interactive graphic interface, where different colours indicate different velocities, and the invisible eddies and turbulences of fluid dynamics become visible. The possibilities these tools afford the designer for a better understanding of the relationship between built form and environment are exciting – where surface morphology of a building skin can help to drive natural ventilation and cooling.

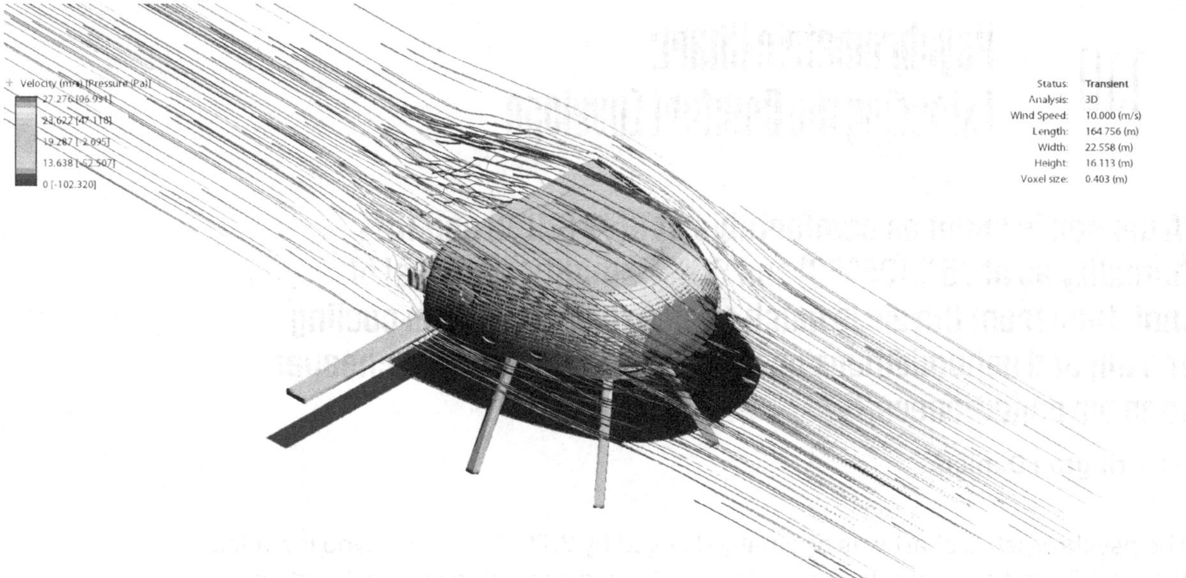

↑ **Fig 1.09.1** Iteration 5, CFD study of the Warbler Housing Pod, part of the Doggerville self-sustainable island near East Tilbury designed by Rupert Heasman.

↓ **Fig 1.09.2** Iteration 6, CFD study of the Warbler Housing Pod'.

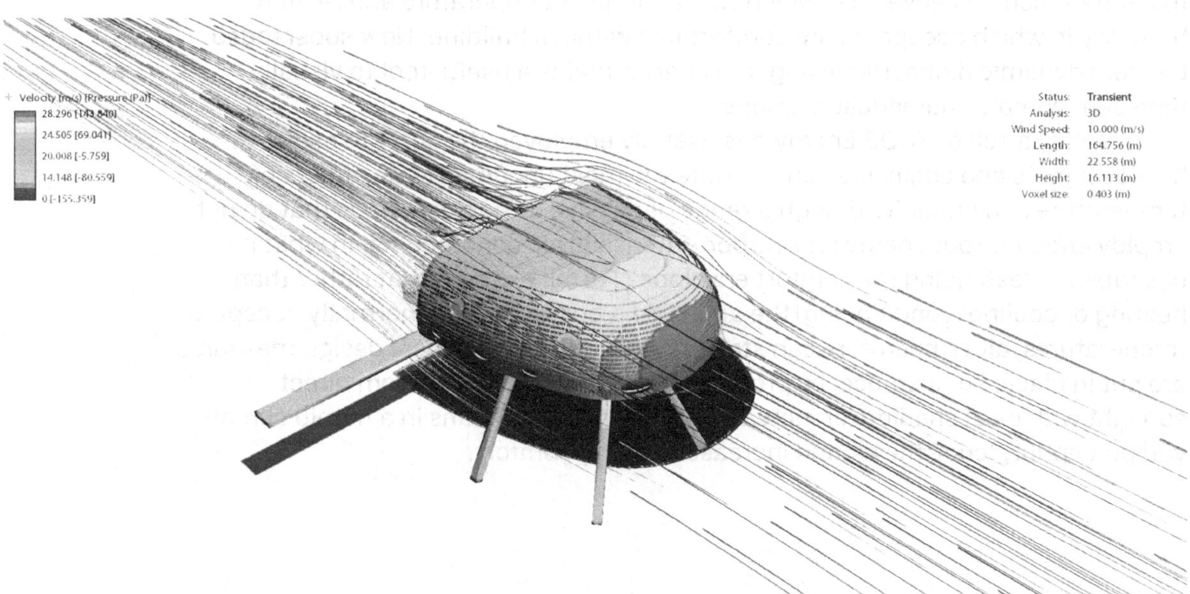

1.10 Psychrometric Chart: Extending the Comfort Envelope

'A person is about as comfortable at 85°F (29°C) and 10% humidity as at 75°F (24° FC) and 80% humidity. Removal of moisture from the air is much easier to achieve than cooling the air, and dehumidifiers operated by electricity are cheaper than air conditioners.'[22]

– Farrington Daniels

The psychrometric chart was originally devised by Willis H. Carrier, who installed the world's first air-conditioning system in 1903, designed to control building humidity. The chart, originally described as the hygrometric chart when it was first published in 1905, was designed as a visual aid to understanding the thermodynamic parameters of moisture in air at a constant pressure. The key properties represented are wet bulb temperature (the lowest temperature at which any fluid can be cooled), dry bulb temperature (the typical measure of air temperature recorded by a thermometer exposed to the air, but shielded from radiation and moisture) and absolute and relative humidity and enthalpy (the energy content of air). The chart enabled engineers to understand the interdependent relationship between all of these psychrometric factors and to define a 'comfort envelope', which was a range of temperature and related humidity in which occupants are comfortable within a building. Now superseded by more dynamic digital modelling, the chart remains a useful tool to visually represent complex numerical relations.

John Farrell of XCO2 Energy has usefully employed the chart to explain how designers and engineers can mitigate the most uncomfortable effects of temperature and humidity though a range of passive design measures that do not employ effective (but energy and carbon-intensive) air-conditioning. In what he describes as 'extending the comfort envelope', Farrell explains that rather than heating or cooling (conditioning) the air inside a building within normally accepted temperatures, air temperature can stray beyond this range if local design measures are put in place. For instance, by protecting building occupants from direct sunlight with local shading, or increasing air velocity with fans in a humid climate, you perceptibly 'cool' the air and increase building comfort.

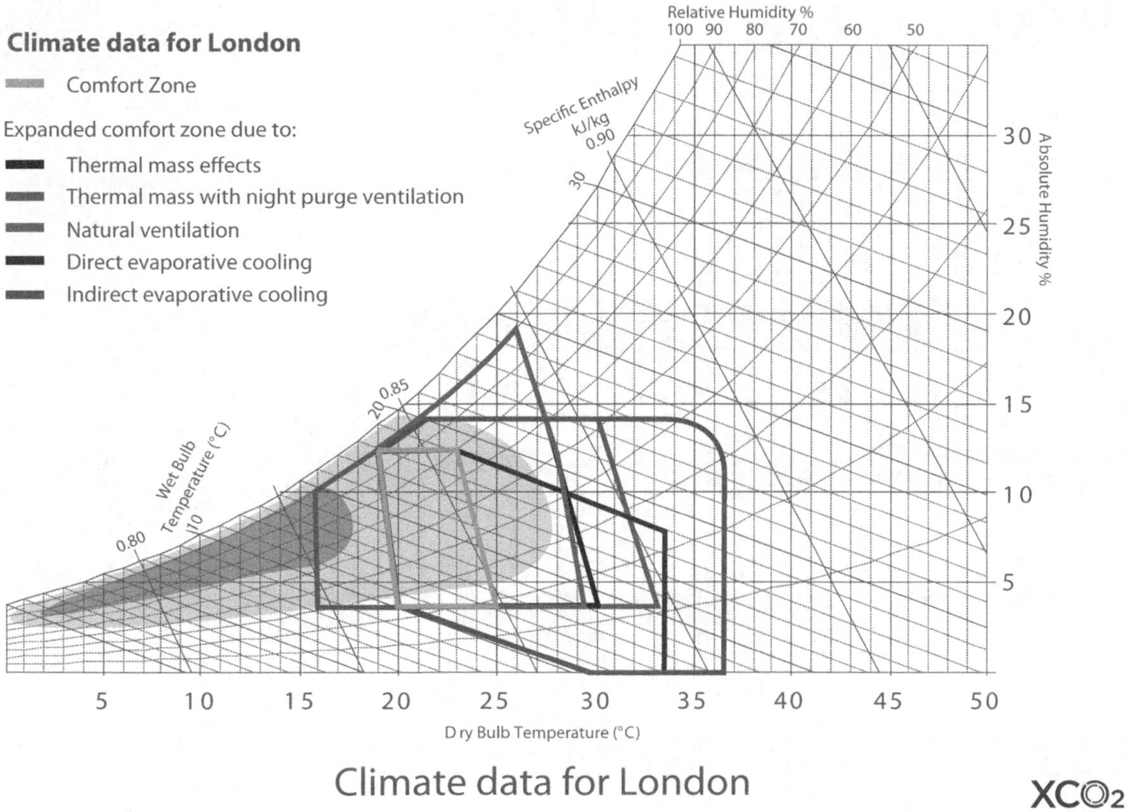

↑ **Fig 1.10.1** The psychrometric chart for London as annotated by John Farrell, showing how through a series of passive (low-energy) strategies we can extend the 'comfort envelope' of buildings.
John Farrell – XCO2.

‘Fossil fuels will one day give way to renewable energy. That means we need to find new material systems that are not petroleum-based. I believe that those material systems will be biological, but what matters is how we design and build them.’[23]

Natsai Audrey Chieza

Chapter 2
Materials Technology

While the banning of concrete and its energy-intensive 'magic' ingredient of cement might be excellent for the CO_2 balance sheet and thus climate change, what would replace this versatile, strong and fireproof material? Steel and aluminium are energy-intensive to produce from the raw mined materials of iron ore and bauxite, respectively, but they are endlessly recyclable. Whether we still need to mine for these raw materials is another question. Buckminster Fuller, as part of his World Design Decade project in the early 1960s, made the point that there was more iron ore out of the ground in the form of steel than remained to be mined. With careful upcycling and recycling of metals, using improved 'waste' supply chains and electric arc furnaces powered by sustainable sources, might we provide all the metals we need, with an end to mining? Interestingly, the only aluminium smelting plant left in the UK is powered by hydroelectric power, so while this is a hugely energy-intense process, to what extent can its carbon footprint be mitigated? If the production of cement is powered by sustainable sources, and the carbon emissions associated with its production can be sequestered back into that material, then are we getting somewhere?

Design and construction have a set of conflicting criteria, and there is no single 'right' answer. The designer should therefore inform themselves about client, site, cost, material availability and proximity, and the cost (financial, social and environmental) of all design choices.

In this chapter on materials technology, we highlight new developments in cement replacement materials as well as the properties of lime – the precursor to cement, less energy-intensive to produce, but with a host of material properties and uses within construction. New ideas of 'biofabrication' are discussed, with the potential of the cultivated substrates of mushrooms as mycelium building blocks and/or thermal insulation. Hempcrete is also a compelling construction material that uses the cheapest 'waste' component of a farmed crop in combination with lime. It is currently being produced in block form by a traditional English brickworks that has risen to the challenge of climate change, and understands the dynamic interplay of fabrication and production and the semi-agricultural traditions of the brick industry. Meanwhile Shigeru Ban demonstrates the inventive reuse or technology transfer of the cardboard tube – pioneered by the packaging industry, but usefully employed in large and small-scale structures, with Ban singlehandedly reviving the use of paper as a construction material. There is an emphasis on 'natural' or non-fossil fuel bio-polymers in the work of iconoclast artist and inventor Zbigniew Oksiuta, and in John Hutchinson's piece on fibre-reinforced polymer (FRP) composites, he highlights how early high-strength composite materials utilised natural fibres (hemp, jute, etc.) and plant oil-based resins in their manufacture. The rediscovery of these technologies in response to climate change and material provenance is both encouraging and inspiring, and should motivate designers to better understand the biological and structural properties of materials and make informed choices for their appropriate use. With the work of both Chris Leung and Doris Sung, we see how the natural properties of a material (or bi-material, in the case of Sung) can be harnessed to create a thermally dynamic surface that can provide shade and insulation in direct, passive-powered thermal response.

As a designer, one of your important roles is as a specifier, and the more you understand about materials and their appropriate use with respect to safety and weathering, the more likely it is that a project can meet specific programmatic, technical and environmental objectives. A renewed interest in the provenance and local sourcing of materials may also form part of an initial design process, or at least the design brief. The sourcing of raw or reclaimed materials, labour and the associated supply chain could form part of a virtuous circle of economic and social, as well as ecological, sustainability.

The potential of new plant-based materials such as mycelium or hemp present the designer with an exciting and expanded store cupboard of sustainable building materials. The interesting experimental work that specialist brick maker H.G. Matthews is doing with lightweight hempcrete blocks is born of an environmental consciousness as well as the need to develop new business and products. The work of Biohm with mycelium exploits the natural thermal insulative properties of this natural medium while utilising waste products from other industries such as agriculture or packaging in its production. Biohm is currently undertaking technical testing and accreditation of these new plant-based products, bringing these seemingly niche products into mainstream construction.

↑ Fig 2.00.1 Glass brick paver made from waste crushed glass cullet fused and moulded in a small kiln. Green Bottle Unit/Eluna 2005. Glass is endlessly recyclable and British Glass explain that for every tonne of glass re-melted 246 kg of carbon dioxide emissions will be saved compared with the manufacture of new glass from raw mined materials.

2.01	**Bio-Polymer: Made of Air**
	Designers: Allison Dring and Daniel Schwaag – Made of Air

‘Making CO_2 from the atmosphere a usable material.’[24]

– Allison Dring

Made of Air (MOA) is a new biochar-based material designed to combat climate change. MOA is made from 90% atmospheric carbon, and the material is designed as a sustainable alternative to timber and composite panels for use in construction, interiors, furniture and product design. MOA is carbon negative: its production removes more CO_2 from the air than it emits. The material is fabricated from biochar, a carbon-rich substance similar to charcoal that is produced by the pyrolysis (oxygen-free baking) of waste biomass from forestry and agriculture. Biochar is currently used in agriculture as a soil improver, helping the soil to better retain nutrients and moisture. The carbon captured by the biomass during photosynthesis (as plants and trees) is subsequently sequestered in the biochar. For every tonne of MOA produced, its makers explain that 2.5 tonnes of CO_2 are sequestered, and it will generate 3.6 MWh of energy during its production.

The material is energy net positive, as the pyrolysis process releases heat energy, which if used in combination with a combined heat and power (CHP) plant can store the heat or convert it into electrical energy. This new construction material can be technically described as a bio-thermoplastic, and is easily moulded, formed and machined. MOA is non-toxic and is made from 90% biochar and a small amount of a plant-based bio-polymer as a binding agent. MOA is fully recyclable, and at the end of its life cycle can be collected, recycled and reformed into new products. Alternatively, this fossil fuel-free material can be safely landfilled. MOA is currently being manufactured in Germany.

Made of Air is based in Berlin, and was founded in 2016 by architect Allison Dring and materials specialist Daniel Schwaag. Their company Elegant Embellishments produces custom facades that actively neutralise urban pollutants such as nitrous oxide (see also page 99).

→ **Fig 2.01.1** Acoustic panels fabricated from sequestered carbon. This prototype panel by Made of Air is made from a non-fossil fuel thermoplastic using biochar.

2.02	**Bio-Polymer: Spatium Gelatum**
	Designer: Zbigniew Oksiuta

'... I was interested in expanding the term architecture. There is something like pure architecture. Like searching for a space in which you can enclose yourself, separated from everything else, and survive due to the temperature, due to privacy.'[25]

– Zbigniew Oksiuta

Zbigniew Oksiuta is an artist, architect and scientist who has been designing and researching experimental biological structures for almost 30 years. Oksiuta argues that most of what has been described as organic, fluid or dynamic architecture is no such thing, and its relationship with biology is analogical at best. His Spatium Gelatum project was designed to explore new forms of architecture that could provide environmental enclosure made from a calorific substance that could also feed its inhabitants. Oksiuta is interested in the relationship between architecture and the biological sciences, and Spatium Gelatum was designed to create different climatic conditions, tastes and smells. In order to fabricate these complex spatial forms, Oksiuta has examined the concept of isopycnic systems and neutral buoyancy (lava lamp technology), and in 2004 he created a large bio-polymer structure underwater at the European Space Agency's neutral buoyancy facility.

Oksiuta acknowledged Frei Otto's work and what Otto describes as a 'Pneu'[26] or pneumatic construction as one of nature's fundamental construction technologies. Initial prototypes have been fabricated with the biological polymer by-product gelatine, and agar jelly made from algae. These structures have then been formed with the use of air, with an inflatable formwork of air directly injected into the material, like bubblegum. Oksiuta's work with natural polymers has presaged a huge new interest in the constructional possibilities of a non-fossil fuel thermoplastics and composites.

In 2007, Oksiuta presented a version of his research entitled Biological Habitat, which showed his futuristic vision of inhabitable forms that could be germinated and grown like plants. The bubble structures would be made from a bio-polymer and could expand to the size of a house, and after hardening the bio-polymer skin would become as strong as concrete and as transparent as glass. The habitat was also designed to float on water. Oksiuta's ambition is not simply to create a new home or shelter, but to create a whole life support system.

↑ Fig 2.02.1 Zbigniew Oksiuta inside one of his bio-polymer Spatium Gelatum structures, 2004.

2.03 Cement Replacement Materials

'The chemical and thermal combustion processes involved in the production of cement are a large source of carbon dioxide (CO_2) emissions. Each year, more than 4 billion tonnes of cement are produced, accounting for around 8 per cent of global CO_2 emissions.'[27]

– Johanna Lehne and Felix Preston

The quest for cement-less concrete proves elusive. The process of making Portland cement, which forms the 'glue' in concrete, requires heating limestone, clay and shale at 1450°C to create clinker, which is then cooled and ground to a fine powder. The embodied energy generated by its production is a huge source of CO_2 emissions, and there are many researchers and industry bodies actively engaged with the removal of and/or the reduction of cement content in concrete. However, reinforced concrete is a wonderful construction material: its strength, fire resistance and thermal properties as a heavy mass material (it can store heat and coolth) are hard to dispense with. While cement reduction and removal are one means of reducing embodied energy and therefore CO_2, there are other factors to consider. We can mitigate the use of reinforced concrete by employing its mass for heat storage and transfer, as seen in Atelier Ten's Thermal Labyrinth technology (see page 124) and Skanska's Energy Pile technology (see page 116). We can also minimise the amount of concrete used by creating thin reinforced concrete shells, for example in the work of Dante Bini (see page 78), where he removes the need for costly formwork by using air and lightweight fabrics as formwork. There is also the question of optimised structural engineering solutions and whether we actually need to pour large amounts of concrete into the ground to provide foundations for small buildings (see Cork House, page 136).

For cement replacement materials, there is renewed interest in volcanic ash, where the super-heating of rock has provided the stone with pozzolanic properties, which the Romans usefully employed in the wondrous (unreinforced) concrete of the Pantheon in Rome. Other common cement replacement materials are typically used to replace a proportion of the total Portland cement, but cannot be used to entirely replace the cement because of strength and setting times. Cement replacement materials are typically the waste by-products of other industrial processes and include pulverised fuel ash (PFA or fly ash), a by-product of coal-fired power stations; ground granulated blast-furnace slag (GGBS), a by-product of the steel industry, and silica fume, a by-product from the manufacture of silicon. Of course, the phasing-out of coal-fired power stations will eventually end the production of PFA, and the steel industry is moving towards a more widespread use of electric arc furnaces that recycle existing steel rather than make new steel from mined iron ore. A more recent addition to the stable of cement replacement materials is domestic waste sludge powder (DWSP) from human waste, of which there is a plentiful supply, and Thames Water is currently supplying DWSP for the production of concrete building blocks.

Another means to reduce or even eliminate the carbon footprint of cement would be to replace the energy source required to produce cement in the first place with renewable sources such as sunlight. US startup Heliogen is using arrays of sun-tracking heliostats to concentrate sunlight and produce carbon-free energy for industrial uses such as the production of cement. In a recent innovation CarbonCure has found a way to sequester the CO_2 produced by manufacturing cement – by injecting it into concrete, which forms a calcium carbonate permanently locked into the concrete matrix.

↑ Fig 2.03.1 Heliogen's commercial facility in Lancaster, California, which has managed to concentrate solar energy to exceed temperatures greater than 1000°C.

→→ Fig 2.03.2 Drone image of Heliogen commercial facility, showing the heliostat array.

2.04

Composites – Fibre-Reinforced Polymers

By John Hutchinson, Ecos Maclean

'... not only should it never be necessary to consign any composite to land-fill when it has reached the end of its allotted service life, but also there are now always available good and cost-effective options for materials retrieval and re-use.'

– John Hutchinson

The first modern composites – i.e. matrix resin reinforced with strong fibres – were largely sourced from naturally occurring materials. There is a famous picture from around 80 years ago of Henry Ford II standing over the boot of a Ford Model A wielding a fire axe to demonstrate the toughness of the natural fibre-reinforced composite it was made of. *Flight* magazine of January 1946 carries an article about Gordon Aerolite, a crude flax fibre-reinforced phenolic composite intended to be used in place of scarce aluminium for the manufacture of aeroplane fuselage panels. Body panels for the now-notorious East German Trabant 'people's car' consisted of phenolic resin synthesised from coal tar reinforced with cotton.

Commercial development of fibre-reinforced polymer (FRP), in which the matrix resin was derived from the chemical processing of refined crude oil, did not gain any real momentum until the early 1960s. The first commercial applications were in boat building and making car bodies. Composite applications in aerospace did not begin in earnest until the emergence of very strong, lightweight composites reinforced with carbon fibre.

Despite the strength-to-weight advantage of many composites, plus the fact that they are fatigue resistant and do not corrode, use of FRP in construction did not begin until around 1970. And over the last fifty years, and despite many technical developments and refinements, composites have yet to gain any significant penetration into the UK construction market.

The palette of materials available for composite fabrication is huge. Even for processing at the manufacturing stage, there are a number of options: hand lay-up, spray lay-up, vacuum bag moulding, filament winding, press-moulding, pre-preg and pultrusion.

There is also a wide choice of synthetic reinforcement fibres, not only various grades of glass – available as mats, tow, yarns, rovings or 3D textiles – but also reinforcements made of basalt, boron, aromatic polyamide (aramid or Kevlar) and carbon fibre. For natural fibre composite manufacture in Europe, two commercial 'bast' fibres, flax and hemp, are used to the exclusion of all others. Nettle is the strongest bast fibre but, to date, there are no commercial applications for it. Furthermore, there is a large array of matrix resins available. The best structural performance, greater fire resistance and tolerance of variations in ambient temperature are achieved when the matrix resin hardens irreversibly, as is the case with a thermo-setting polymer. The following are commonly used thermo-setting resins: polyester, phenolic resin, vinyl ester, polyurethane, urethane acrylate and epoxy. Furans are thermo-setting resins sourced from cereal crop waste and not by the chemical processing of fossil fuel. This polymer has chemical and material properties similar to phenolic resin.

Composites can be easily moulded to any required shape. They have good thermal resistance (between 16 and 20 times better than stainless steel), better chemical resistance than construction metals, better electrical resistance, no liability to corrode and, subject to the application of a well-formulated gel coat, resistance to degradation even when immersed in water. Glass-reinforced polymers can also be fire-protected.

Composites cannot be recycled as easily as metals, which can be melted down and re-formed. However, they offer better recycling possibilities than mass concrete, which can only be broken up into low-grade hardcore. It should be emphasised here that, not only should it never be necessary to consign any composite to landfill when it has reached the end of its allotted service life, there are now always good and cost-effective options available for materials retrieval and reuse.

↑ **Fig 2.04.1** Henry Ford showing the strength of bio-composite materials by hitting the soybean and hemp composite boot of his car with an axe, 1940.

↑ Fig 2.04.2 Bio-composite tessellated vault prototypes made from woven hemp fibre and bio-resin (a plant-oil based epoxy). The folded edge flanges provide additional structural stiffness as well as excellent structural connections. Guy Sinclair, research associate at the Fabrication Laboratory, University of Westminster.

→ Fig 2.04.3 These bio-composite panels are translucent as well as structurally rigid. Guy Sinclair, research associate at the Fabrication Laboratory, University of Westminster.

2.05	**Heat Motors**
	Designer/Researcher: Dr Christopher Leung

'The prospect of a building envelope that could physically reconfigure itself with a variety of appropriate responses to seasonal changes in its surrounding environment for improved envelope performance has inspired architects to investigate facade designs with movable elements.'[28]

–Christopher Leung

Architect and academic Christopher Leung has carried out research into environmentally responsive architecture for over two decades. His research is driven by exploring the interrelationship between building, climate and occupant. In his doctoral thesis, Leung investigated the use of heat motors as a passive means to physically move a building's facade construction to regulate its thermal performance and improve human comfort. Leung defines a heat motor as an actuator that converts thermal energy to mechanical energy. Importantly, heat motors operate passively, relying solely on thermal energy from the sun and ambient air temperature, without the need for any external power source.

A heat motor consists of a cylinder filled with wax and sealed with a 'piston' that reciprocates linearly depending on the state of the wax. Wax is a PCM – when it absorbs enough sensible and latent heat to reach its melting point temperature it becomes liquid and expands between 10 and 20% by volume. The wax expansion behind the piston provides a large physical force that, when coupled to suitable mechanisms, is sufficient to open windows, shutters or ventilators. This technology has existed for over 50 years and is widely used in greenhouses to operate ventilators for regulating internal temperature. The mechanical actuation of a heat motor reciprocates when the temperature of the wax cools to its melting point, when it solidifies and shrinks in volume, with the dead weight of the ventilator compressing the wax and allowing the ventilator to close. The operating temperature (the point at which actuation occurs) of a heat motor can be 'tuned' by using a pure paraffin or a blend of wax PCMs with a melting point ranging from -10 to 45°C.

The potential of this proven technology is significant when we consider that heat motors might not simply open a vent,[29] but might also control solar shading or deploy thermal insulation to store or release building heat as necessary.[30] The self-regulatory or homeostatic behaviour of wax and similar materials suggests an architecture that can respond to changes in the diurnal or seasonal environmental conditions. It could physically reconfigure building-scale components, and do so entirely passively without the need for a fossil-fuel energy source or electronic control system.

↑ **Fig 2.05.1** Deployable external insulation demonstration pavilion in UCL quadrangle, by Professor Stephen Gage with Christopher Leung, Nicholas Browne, Fred Guttfield and Joe Moorehouse, 2009.

→ **Fig 2.05.2** Kielder survey probe – heat-motor operated device, sixteen*(makers), Kielder Forest, 2006.

2.06	**Hempcrete**
	Manufacturers: UK Hempcrete and H.G. Matthews

'Hempcrete is unique in this mixture of insulation and thermal mass. In natural building terms, it can be thought of as halfway between straw bale (which has loads of insulation, but very little thermal mass) and cob (which has loads of thermal mass and very little insulation).'[31]

– UK Hempcrete

Hempcrete is made from a mixture of hemp shiv (the hard stems of the industrial hemp plant) with a hydraulic lime binding agent. The lime binder will typically contain a small amount of Portland cement or a pozzolanic cement replacement material (see page 38). Industrial hemp is a fast-growing plant that matures in as little as 8–12 weeks and can be farmed across the world except in arid areas. It can be used in the production of paper, textiles, bioplastics, health supplements and fuel. It is also rich in cellulose, proteins and oils, but does not contain the psychoactive compound THC. The shiv stems were traditionally the low-value component of hemp and were seen as a waste product. Hempcrete can be described as a carbon-negative building material, as the process of growing the plants absorbs high levels of CO_2 and, even accounting for the binding materials, transportation and construction, it will store more CO_2 than it takes for its production.

Hempcrete can be used as a liquid slurry and cast into a formwork or formed into lightweight blocks. The material is not typically used as a load-bearing material, and is usually built around a timber frame or used as an infill material for external and internal walls. Hempcrete is a hygroscopic material that can absorb humidity from the air and then re-release it, regulating internal air properties and air quality. It is a non-toxic material that does not emit harmful volatile organic compounds (VOCs).

H.G. Matthews is a traditional, handmade brickworks in Buckinghamshire. Alongside its wood-fired clay bricks it also manufactures unfired straw and clay blocks (Strocks), and has recently started producing hempcrete blocks using hemp from its own farmland. The process of forming the lightweight hempcrete blocks requires no more complicated machinery than a series of moulds and labour, and the blocks are air dried. The density of the blocks is 280 kg/m^3 (half the weight of a comparable aircrete block) with a thermal conductivity 0.076 W/m^{2}K. UK Hempcrete, one of the UK's leading hempcrete specialists, explains that the typical thickness of a newbuild hempcrete wall is 300–400 mm, with typical U-values of 0.2 W/m^{2}K at 300 mm thickness, 0.17 W/m^{2}K at 350 mm thickness and 0.15 W/m^{2}K at 400 mm thickness.

↑ Fig 2.06.1 Hempcrete blocks being fabricated in timber moulds at H.G. Matthews Brickworks, Buckinghamshire, 2019.

↑ **Fig 2.06.2** Hempcrete infill wall in English oak frame. The Hempcrete wall is cast in situ and can be internally finished with a lime or clay plaster and externally finished with a lime plaster.
UK Hempcrete.

→ **Fig 2.06.3** A Hempcrete wall being cast in situ. The timber shuttering shown is lightweight because of the relative low density of the Hempcrete. UK Hempcrete.

2.07	Lime
	By John Hutchinson, Ecos Maclean

'Any concerns about its suitability as a material for bedding and jointing load-bearing brickwork should be dispelled by the fact that its long use throughout the last two thousand years has proved that it is strong enough to support structures such as Salisbury cathedral spire, the ducal palace in Urbino and the Pantheon in Rome.'

– John Hutchinson

Lime as a binding medium has several advantages over the strong material that has tended to usurp it in construction, ordinary Portland cement. All of these uses of lime offer environmental benefits when compared to conventional cement mixes. Below is a short guide to the properties and qualities of lime as part of the construction process, describing its chemistry, 'fattening up', carbon footprint, long-term durability and strength.

Simple chemistry

Lime is chemically simple. Calcium carbonate ($CaCO_3$) in the form of limestone lumps is burned at around 800°C and reduced to calcium oxide (CaO). The burned material is then 'slaked' by adding water. This makes a lively and exothermic (heat-emitting) chemical reaction in which the oxide is hydrated to become calcium hydroxide ($Ca(OH)_2$). This white, putty-like substance has been used traditionally as binder in lime mortar, plaster, render and, occasionally, lime concrete.

Fattening up

Research has identified two nano-scale forms of calcium hydroxide. One is a prismatic particle. The other is a flat, almost two-dimensional hexagon. The latter has the property of attracting water molecules that attach to the corners of the hexagon. Lime obtained as putty has been observed to contain more hexagonal platelets than lime in the form of dry hydrate packed in bags. If the putty is agitated, the platelets acquire their water molecule attachments, which imbue the putty with a lubricating, oily character. This makes so-called 'fat' lime very easy to work with and to place neatly in a brick or masonry joint. The agitation is referred to as 'knocking up' on UK building sites.

Carbon footprint

Lime has a superior carbon footprint to cement. When limestone is burned, CO_2 is released into the air not only from the burning fuel, but also from the limestone. However, the CO_2 emitted from the limestone will normally find its way back, provided that the mortar, plaster or render is open to air circulation and exposed to wetting and drying out. The process is called 'carbonation'. CO_2 emitted to the air from limestone during burning is later removed from the air as lime carbonates. Lime binder in any building material exposed to rainfall will almost always revert back to calcium carbonate over time.

Long-term durability

Although lime mortar, gauged in the customary ratio of one part lime to three parts aggregate, is nowhere near as strong as a cement mortar after curing (in the range of one-tenth to one-fifteenth of the compression strength of a 1:6 cement mortar after 28 days), the consequences of carbonation and long-term crystal formation are that the mortar will very gradually gain strength. Lime mortar that has been left undisturbed in a masonry or brick wall not exposed to sulphuric acid in rain for more than a century is likely to resist decay or degradation for at least another century.

Strength in use

The compression strength of lime and the mortar or mass concrete made with it varies according to what type and shape of aggregate was used (sharp, well-graded aggregate makes stronger mortar), how much water was present in the mix (too much makes it weaker), the skill of the tradesperson preparing and placing the material, and the exposure after completion of the work to the vagaries of the weather. Charles Barry's Gothic Palace of Westminster ascends from a 1.50 m deep lime concrete slab for which the binding medium was feeble hydraulic lime procured mostly from quarries near Reigate on the North Downs. The life expectancy of this lime concrete can therefore be reliably claimed to be indefinite.

← **Fig 2.07.1** Traditional (slaked) lime wash or 'cal' as used in Menorca to protect the stone. Used inside and out, the coating produces a bright surface glow due to the refraction of the calcite crystals. Lime wash is applied in very thin layers, is antimicrobial and helps to resist insects, and is breathable.

2.08	**Mycelium Biofabrication**
	Designers: Biohm, David Benjamin - The Living

'Biofabrication: literally fabricating with biology ... instead of processing plants, animals or oil to make consumer materials, we might grow materials directly with living organisms. In what many are terming "the Fourth Industrial Revolution", we're thinking about the new factories as being living cells. Bacteria, algae, fungi, yeast: our latest design tools include those of biotechnology.'[32]

– Suzanne Lee

Mycelium is the mass of fibrous threads that forms the vegetative part of a fungus. Mycelium behaves in a similar way to yeast, producing enzymes that break down and absorb the natural sugars of waste products such as wood shavings, plant waste and spent coffee grounds. By 'feeding' on this waste, the mycelium grows a compact mesh of fibres (the root structures of a mushroom) that can be trained around the 'food' substrate and grown into a sheet material or into a shaped mould, by controlling the temperature and humidity. Different types of fungi can be selected and refined to adjust the properties of the resultant material, such as elasticity or hardness. These materials are grown rather than wrought from inert materials, and once the material has reached the required size and before it becomes a mushroom proper, the mycelium is heat-treated to kill the micro-organisms. This fixes the material's size and properties.

Mycelium is fast-growing and carbon neutral, with some excellent material properties. It has been used as lightweight packaging to replace petrochemical-based expanded foams, and as thermal insulation material. London-based biomaterial specialist Biohm explains that its mycelium insulation panels are able to achieve a thermal conductivity of 0.024 W/m²K, better than materials such as glass fibre (0.032–0.044 W/m²K), mineral wool (0.032–0.044 W/m²K), expanded polystyrene (0.036 W/m²K) and extruded polystyrene (0.029–0.036 W/m²K). Mycelium has also been developed as a leather-like fabric for shoes, as well as a foodstuff in the form of Quorn, which was devised in the 1960s (and has been on sale since 1985) as a protein-rich meat substitute. The process of mycelium manufacture is not energy-intensive and does not require heavy plant and machinery, and as such could be classified as a 'light' industrial process akin to running a large bakery.

In 2014, a team led by David Benjamin from the design practice The Living built Hy-Fi, a 12 m high tower, from 10,000 mycelium bricks at MoMA PS1 art centre in Queens, New York City. The bricks were manufactured by Ecovative from a mycelium matrix grown from corn stalks, and they were stacked to form three interlocking tubes. Arup provided structural engineering support, and the blocks were structurally tested at Columbia University and proved more than capable of resisting the necessary compressive loads. While it might be that a fully-fledged mycelium building is more an exemplary than a ubiquitous construction type, the closed-loop upcycling of 'waste' material, which the growth (commodity and actual) supports is impressive.

↑ **Fig 2.08.1** Using agricultural waste and mycelium cultures, London-based designer and carbon neutral material specialist Biohm has developed a panel-based mycelium, which is lightweight and has excellent thermal properties.

↑ Fig 2.08.2 Hy-Fi 12 m high tower made from mycelium bricks.
David Benjamin and The Living, New York City, 2014.

HY-FI
BRICK STACKING AND ASSEMBLY

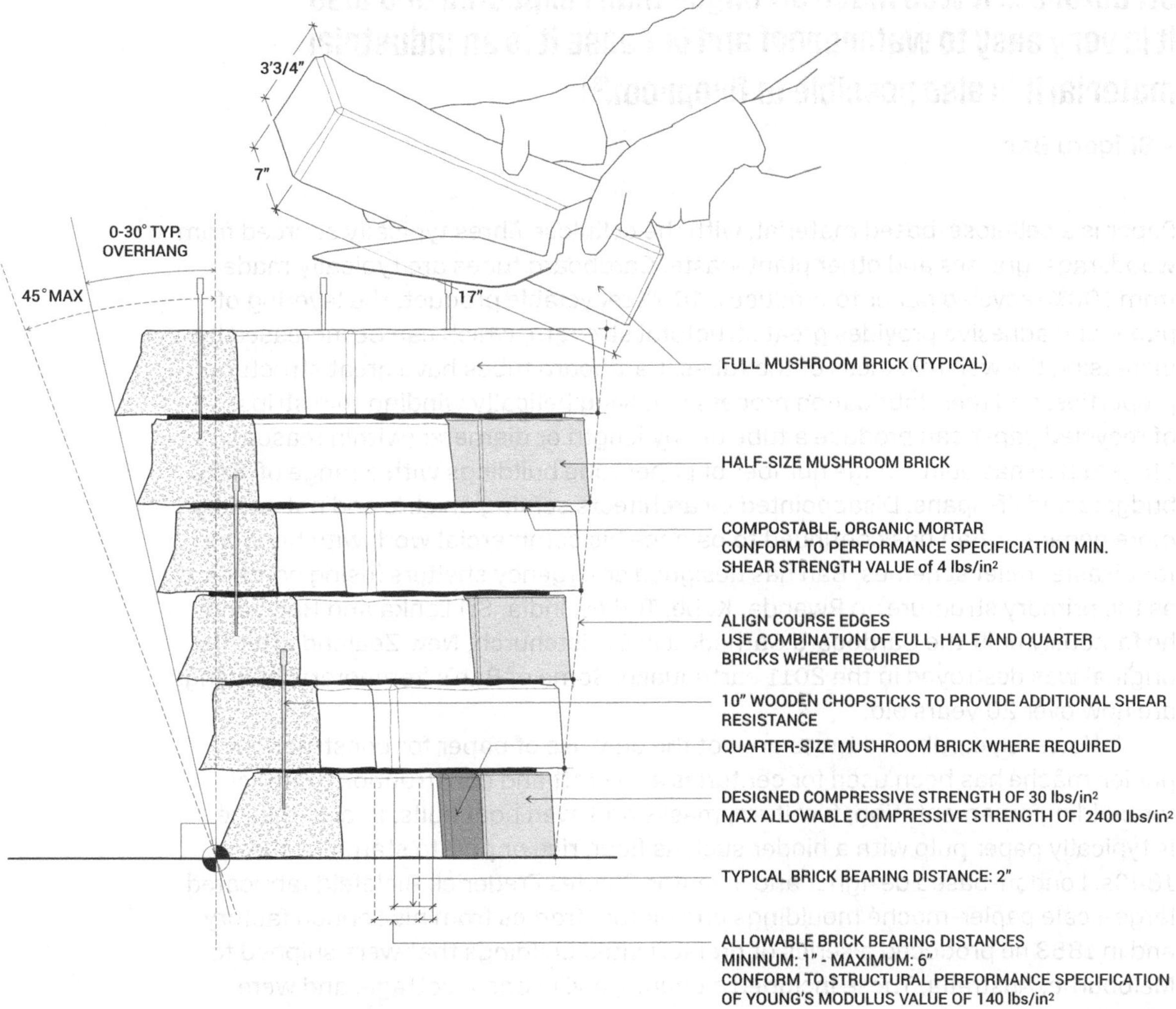

↑ **Fig 2.08.3** Hy-Fi tower, mycelium brick stacking and assembly diagram. Dimensions are imperial. David Benjamin and The Living, New York City, 2014.

2.09	**Paper Buildings**
	Designers: Shigeru Ban, i/thee and Roundhouse Platform

'I started testing the paper tubes to use as a building structure ... it was much stronger than I expected and also it is very easy to waterproof and because it is an industrial material it is also possible to fireproof.'[33]

– Shigeru Ban

Paper is a cellulose-based material, with the cellulose fibres typically sourced from wood, rags, grasses and other plant waste. Cardboard tubes are typically made from 100% recycled paper to produce a 100% recyclable product, the layering of paper and adhesive provides great structural strength, which can be increased by increasing the wall thickness of the tubes. Cardboard tubes have great structural properties, and their fabrication process involving helically winding thin strips of recycled paper can produce a tube of any length or diameter (within reason). Shigeru Ban has built a huge number of paper tube buildings with a range of sizes, budgets and lifespans. Disappointed by architects serving an elite and not society more generally, Ban has continued to balance his commercial work with his work for disaster relief schemes. Ban has designed emergency shelters (using cardboard as the primary structure) in Rwanda, Kobe, Turkey, India, Sri Lanka and Haiti, and he famously built the Cardboard Cathedral in Christchurch, New Zealand after the original was destroyed in the 2011 earthquake. Some of Ban's 'temporary' buildings are now over 20 years old.

However, cardboard tubes are not the only use of paper for construction; papier-mâché has been used for centuries as a craft and construction material for building ornamentation, furniture, masks and even boat hulls. Papier-mâché is typically paper pulp with a binder such as flour, rice or potato starch. In the 1840s, London-based designer and inventor Charles Frederick Bielefeld fabricated large-scale papier-mâché mouldings and picture frames from his London factory, and in 1853 he produced a series of prefabricated buildings that were shipped to Melbourne, Australia. These included a church, a villa and a cottage, and were fabricated in a series of panels designed to be bolted together. The projects were published in 1853, in a catalogue produced by his eponymous company entitled 'Portable Buildings'. The *Illustrated London News* featured the project and reported that the buildings had been shipped to Melbourne after testing in the English weather of Staines. Harriet Hawkes explains the industrialisation of his fabrication processes: 'His layered papers by this time were allowed to dry naturally, before being oil-saturated and dried a second time in stoves.'[34] Bielefeld's papier-mâché was famously used for the ceiling of Sydney Smirke's reading room at the British Library (now the British Museum).

↑ Fig 2.09.1 Cardboard Cathedral by Shigeru Ban in Christchuch, New Zealand. The roof structure is made from cardboard tubes, as is the cross, lecturn and altar.

← **Fig 2.09.2** The rose window of the Cardboard Cathedral by Shigeru Ban in Christchuch, New Zealand.

In 2020, the design/build studio i/thee, in collaboration with Roundhouse Platform, created the Agg Hab (Aggregate Habitat), a prototypical eco-dwelling in Clarendon, Texas. The structure was formed by casting papier-mâché strips into sculpted holes in the ground. Measuring over 6 m long, 2.5 m wide and 1.5 m high (internal height, with excavated ground 3 m), the structure was fabricated using nearly 200 litres of glue and 130 kg of paper. The designers have described the house as one the world's largest self-supporting papier-mâché structures.

← **Fig 2.09.3** Completed Agg Hab structure by i/thee in collaboration with Roundhouse Platform, Texas, 2020.

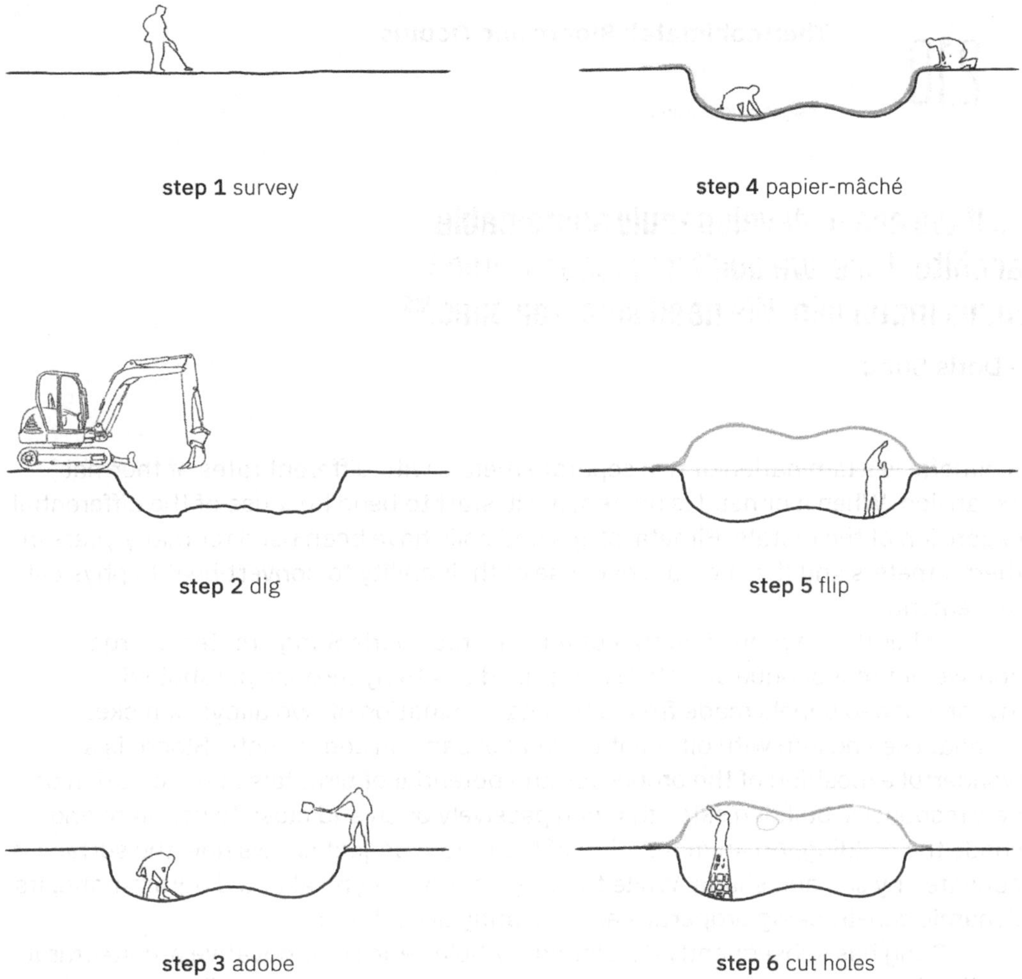

↑ Fig 2.09.4 Agg Hab construction sequence. i/thee in collaboration with Roundhouse Platform.

↓ Fig 2.09.5 Drone footage showing Agg Hab construction process of excavation, papier-mâché moulding, and flipping the paper shell to create a shelter. i/thee in collaboration with Roundhouse Platform.

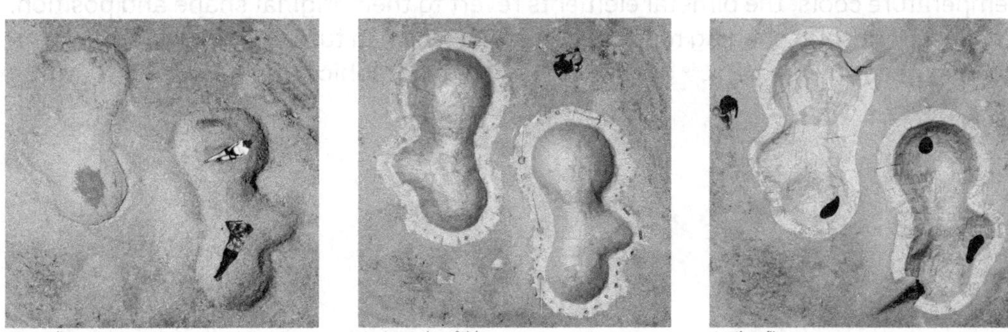

step one dig **step two** papier-mâché **step three** flip

2.10	**Thermobimetal: Bloom and Oculus**
	Designer: Doris Sung

'... if we are to develop truly sustainable architecture, we don't necessarily need more materials. We need smarter ones.'[35]

– Doris Sung

A bimetal is a lamination of two separate metals with different rates of thermal expansion. When a bimetal is heated, it will start to bend because of the differential expansion of the metals. Bimetal strips and coils have been used for many years in thermometers and thermostats because of their ability to convert heat to physical movement.

In her Bloom project, architect and inventor Doris Sung created a large lightweight monocoque structure comprised of 414 hyperbolic paraboloid (hypar) shaped panels made from a bimetal lamination of two alloys of nickel, manganese and iron with different thermal expansion coefficients. Bloom is a wonderful exposition of the properties and potential of bimetals in the creation of new responsive building skins that can passively open and close to ventilate and shade the building. An animated film of the Bloom project shows how the surface is activated by sun and shade. While the project is prototypical and diagrammatic, its dynamic sun-tracking properties are brilliantly articulated.

Sung has subsequently developed a whole series of innovative architectural applications using thermobimetal. Her initial research on self-shading, self-ventilating and self-assembling alongside contemporary fabrication technologies has expanded the physical potential of the material, for example in the twisting and folding of her Oculus prototype, and she has now patented systems that are being commercialised for wider application. Her InVert™ window-shading system incorporates small bimetal 'petals' within a double-glazed glass module, and as the temperature from the sun increases, the bimetal elements deform and block the sunlight and shade the building's interior. As the sunlight moves and the temperature cools, the bimetal elements revert to their original shape and position. The resultant solar shading reduces heat gain, which in turn can reduce artificial cooling needs by 28–42%,[36] depending on the geographical location.

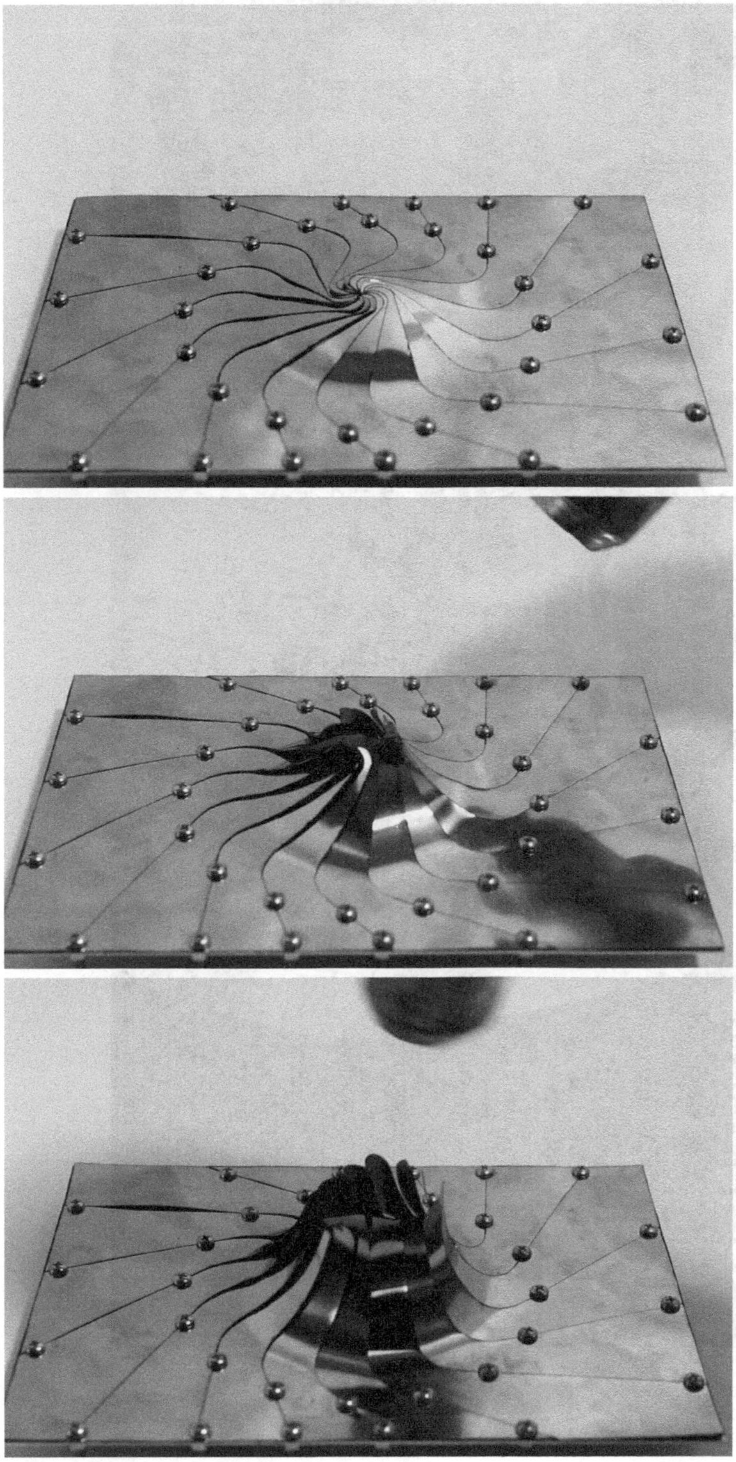

↑ **Fig 2.10.1** Oculus bimetal prototype showing how with the addition of heat a surface can twist and bend, and create an opening in a surface for light or air to pass through. Doris Sung, DOSU Studio Architecture.

↑ **Fig 2.10.2** Completed sun-tracking Bloom canopy project in Los Angeles, 2011. Doris Sung, DOSU Studio Architecture.

↑ Fig 2.10.3 Detail of Bloom showing how the bimetal surface bends when it is heated by the sun. Doris Sung, DOSU Studio Architecture.

‘No examples of innovations in techniques starting in the building industry and spreading to other industries have appeared … the building industry was dependent on other industries for new techniques.’ [37]

Marian Bowley

Chapter 3: Construction Technology

Writing about the development of the steel industry in the 1930s, Marian Bowley described how, at that time, much of the innovation was coming from shipbuilding and associated industries. So, how is it possible to innovate in an industry that Bowley described as 'resistant to change', and how and where does the innovation come from in a contemporary context?

With the imperative of climate change and the acknowledgement of the role design and construction have to play in mitigating the misuse of the world's natural resources, we need to reshape the way we make things as much as we need to think about what those things are. The shift in emphasis from the operational energy 'in use' of a building, to the 'embodied energy' of construction materials, their sourcing, processing, transportation and future reuse is critical to effecting such a positive change.

Every industry and trade body is quick to tell students and designers of the relative and 'unique' environmental benefits of using their given material and construction methodology. And while the designer needs to understand the full range of material and constructional possibilities, they should also be mindful of unintended consequences of their use. When safety, structural efficiency, environmental benefits or otherwise are all considered, it seems highly unlikely that a single material or construction methodology can provide the answer to all the technical, economic and environmental considerations of any given project. As such, the construction technologies included in this chapter simply provide a snapshot of how to use natural (and local) materials, usefully employ contemporary technology, optimise material use and do more with less.

The chapter opens with a re-evaluation of natural materials such as earth and bamboo. Bamboo is a fast-growing, carbon-sequestering material that has been used in construction for centuries and is being adopted by a new generation of designers and builders for its great structural strength and ease of use. Two very different types of earth construction are featured. Rammed earth is ancient, local, abundant, reusable and simple to build. Part of Rowland Keable's approach to the use of rammed earth is the dissemination of technical information, through published standards and construction training. Stéphanie Chaltiel's sprayed earth architecture uses the same material, but in a very different form and with the useful deployment of the latest drone technology.

Dante Bini's Minishell project must surely meet the standard of an enlightened environmental design even with its (minimised) cement content. Bini can be described as an 'innovating entrepreneur',[38] who has spent his professional life working as both an architect and a builder on a whole series of inventions that he describes as 'construction automation'. The Minishell is a small-scale derivative of his emblematic Binishell; this simpler, more compact and extremely fast construction method uses fabric formwork and low-pressure air to lift and form structures. In another inflatable technology, the pneumatic art and architecture of Graham Stevens provides brilliant technical, programmatic and artistic inspiration. The lightweight architecture of membranes and air was developed in earnest from the 1940s, but its history is truncated in the later part of the 20th century. At this time the oil-crisis-led environmental consciousness was seemingly subsumed by an environmentally unconscious Postmodernism.

Specifically related to structural invention, the arched 'tensegrity' canopy by Geoff Morrow's StructureMode, while a relatively small-scale prototype, illustrates the potential of tensegrity structures to 'do more with less'. Morrow's systematic design of the assembly sequence also made it a pleasure to build. In another highly inventive (and prototypical) project, Will Alsop's Neuron Pod in East London demonstrates the relative strength of thin-sheet steel in a rare monocoque building structure. Utilising an approach more familiar in the nautical, aeronautical and automotive industries, the unusual three-dimensional 'developable surface' is made from thin strips of computer numerical control (CNC) cut and formed weathering steel, welded off site into sections to form a doubly curved auditorium that is both lightweight and structurally optimised. In the final example of steel construction, Adam Kalkin takes the reuse of the ubiquitous shipping container and elevates it to a fine art (literally in the case of his Pushbutton House) in his brilliant Quik House family home, an affordable three-bedroom house largely made from a readily available waste industrial product.

In the timber gridshell structures of Frei Otto, small-section sawn timber thinnings are laid in a two-way grid and bent to provide tremendous compressive structural strength with minimal material use. A seemingly audacious construction process that is actually quite straightforward provides huge spans, with virtually no structural depth in the skin at all. The enduring success of Otto's Mannheim timber gridshell should provide an object lesson in design economy. In schools of architecture in the UK, cross-laminated timber (CLT) has recently seemed like the answer to almost every design and construction problem. But as part of a suite of 'engineered timbers' that includes glue-laminated timber (glulam) and laminated veneer lumber (LVL), it really does have the potential to change the way we construct. CLT is a low-carbon (and in fact a carbon-sequestering) material, it is largely non-toxic (depending on adhesives and preservatives) and it is quick, easy and quiet to build with. However, following the Grenfell Tower fire, in which 72 people lost their lives, the use of combustible materials in the external walls of a residential building over 18 m (six storeys) has been effectively outlawed, temporarily halting its inexorable rise as 'the' modern method of construction.

↑ **Fig 3.00.1** Facade retention, Marylebone, London 2015. Facade retention became popular in the 1980s as a means to appease planners by retaining the outer skin of an existing building while entirely re-building the building interior. Facade retention can now also be understood as part of a strategy to reduce the embodied carbon of a construction project.

3.01	Bamboo Construction: San Pablo Primary School 'Eco-Salon'
	Designer/Researcher: Jan Balbaligo

'... green steel of the 21st century'[39]

– Vo Trong Nghia

Bamboo is not a new building material, but given changing environmental design imperatives, this aggressive, fast-growing plant species provides a strong and durable construction material. Bamboo is the largest member of the grass family, and is one of the fastest-growing plants on the planet – Moso bamboo from China can grow up 900 mm per day. Bamboo can be ready for harvest and construction use in three to five years, compared with 20 to 25 years for softwood timber.

Asia is home to the largest resource of bamboo, but bamboo is able to grow on all of the world's continents except Antarctica. Bamboo has great tensile strength and is easily cut and machined. Before its use in construction, bamboo must be treated to protect it against rotting and insects. There are a number of preservation treatments, some of which use heat, such as smoking, curing and burning. A popular natural preservation treatment involves drilling through the diaphragms that internally divide each node and then submersing the bamboo in a bath of water, boric acid and Borax for a week before drying it in the sun.

Bamboo can be used as whole structural elements such as a columns and beam components, or split and made into panels. Bamboo can also be completely broken down into long fibres and used in textile/rope production or fibre-reinforced polymers. Due to the axial nature of the bamboo fibres, bamboo has incredible tensile strength – it is lightweight, but its elasticity is especially useful in seismic zones.

← **Fig 3.01.1** Students learning to build with bamboo on the Bio-Construction Journey at the Cosmic Convergence Festival, Santiago, Guatemala, 2018.

→ **Fig 3.01.2** Construction of the Eco-Salon with bundles of six bamboo poles forming the structural columns, which are mechanically fixed to concrete upstands connected to the existing roof, San Pablo La Laguna, Solalá, Guatemala.

In his PhD thesis investigating the application of bamboo as reinforcement in structural concrete, Alireza Javadian explains that 'Bamboo ... offers high mechanical properties, including tensile strength, which are comparable to some of the available ASTM graded steel reinforcement materials'.[40] His thesis concludes that while the application of natural bamboo as reinforcement in concrete has proven unsuccessful due to problems of environmental degradation, a bamboo-composite reinforcement is a viable (and environmentally sustainable) alternative to steel.

Designer and bamboo builder Jan Balbaligo has worked on a number of temporary festival structures and small school and community buildings. For larger structural applications, she has created 'bundled' columns, by closely packing between two and seven bamboo 'culms', and strapping (or bolting) them together to create larger structural members. Joints can be made by notching and lashing the bamboo members together with rope or wire, and also mechanically fixing though the material with bolts and dowels. In Oscar Hidalgo López's excellent book on the subject, Manual de construcción con bambú,[41] he explains the importance of working with the cellular nature of the material and utilising the local strength of the nodes for fixing.

In January 2020, Jan Balbaligo worked with non-profit arts and social enterprise Cosmic Convergence to complete the Eco-Salon in San Pablo La Laguna, Solalá, Guatemala. The Eco-Salon is a multifunctional indoor space (85 m²) built on top of an existing public school to provide space for music, sports, arts, dance and other activities to complement and enrich the formal education. The building structure is a bamboo framework, with a bamboo lathe (bamboo splits) roof and bamboo split walls with a bajareke (clay and sand) infill. The project was constructed by a team of ten local builders and a collective of 30 volunteers. The lead contractor of the project was Ivan Davila, with Romà Pujol, Sanjita Singh and Sergio Vicente Chipir, a tz'utujl local leading with the bajareke construction. The project was coordinated by Agostino Giannetti and Silvia Zamprogna, and organised by the Cosmic Social Outreach organisation and the non-profit Cosmic Convergence organisation.

↑ **Fig 3.01.3** The roof structure of the Eco-Salon is made from bamboo splits.

← **Fig 3.01.4** Construction of the bajareke walls with bamboo splits horizontally stacked at 150 mm intervals and held to the bamboo frame with thin wire. Bajareke is a mix of 70% clay and 30% sand, plus water. An additional layer of clay is added to the surface, and then two coats of lime render provide a smooth finish.

→ **Fig 3.01.5** View of the bajareke internal walls being completed.

← **Fig 3.01.6** Completed project with the addition of steel windows and door.

3.02	Earthen Architecture: Drone-Sprayed Earth Mortar
	Designer: Stéphanie Chaltiel – MuDD Architects

'The materials of the future are more (like) processes of the future, where we combine light equipment, local materials and recalibration of those tools on site.'[42]

– Stéphanie Chaltiel

French architect and teacher Stéphanie Chaltiel is a great advocate for the use of earth as a construction material. A necessary local substrate that can be sourced around the world, it is healthy, reusable and strong. While the contemporary construction industry has begun to re-assimilate load-bearing rammed earth as a 'known' technology, Chaltiel has experimented with drones to develop new construction processes that use earth as part of matrix to form a composite building skin. Chaltiel has revisited principles of sprayed concrete (also known as shotcrete) using drones fitted with a spraying hose to apply different layers of biomaterials (non-cement-based mortars) on to a light formwork such as a geodesic dome, gridshell or inflatable structure. Her method obviates the need for expensive scaffolding, and appropriates and uniquely adapts emerging drone technology for use in construction.

In prototypes developed for Milan Design Week in 2019, Chaltiel (MuDD) fabricated three prototypes, the largest of which was an 8 m wide shell, and all of which were constructed in three days using drones to spray and lift. The structures were fabricated from lightweight frames made from bundled thin bamboo sections bound together with rope. The drones then draped the frames in fabric and sprayed them. The spraying included an insulating layer made from rice husks, and was finished with a mixture of local earth. Many of Chaltiel's early prototypes use natural-fibre fabric such as woven jute and hemp as the formwork and reinforcement layer. She has also worked with textile designer Jane Scott on three-dimensional knitted surfaces of recycled fabrics (technical textiles) to create more bespoke substrates.

Chaltiel's work with drones has required her to navigate different regulatory domains, including aviation. Subsequent iterations of these prototypes have used a net enclosure (within which the drone is contained) and can be managed under local health and safety regulations. The drone is also physically connected by an umbilical pipe network transferring the liquid earthen slurry from the feeder tanks to the drone-mounted spray nozzle. Chaltiel's new earthen architecture combines the technology of natural mortar mixes of earth, lime, sand, linen fibres, oils and natural pigments with the literally free-flying mobility of the drone to create a new construction system.

↑ **Fig 3.02.1** Completed bamboo frame and jute fabric structure covered with sprayed earth-mortar. Terramia project built for Milan Design Week 2019.

↓ **Fig 3.02.2** A drone spraying wet earth-mortar on to a bamboo frame and jute fabric structure. Terramia project by Stéphanie Chaltiel for Milan Design Week 2019.

3.03

Earthen Architecture: Rammed Earth Construction

Designer: Rowland Keable – Rammed Earth Consulting

'Pisé de terre, the French for rammed earth, is an ancient type of construction. The writings of Pliny state that watch towers of this material constructed by Hannibal were in use 250 years after completion. It was introduced into France by the Romans and later adopted in England.'[43]

– M.C. Betts and T.A.H. Miller

Earth is still the most widely used construction material across the world, and one of the oldest. Large parts of the Great Wall of China were constructed from earth, and in most parts of the globe there is some kind of earth construction tradition. Earth can be used as bricks, adobe, cob (a mixture of earth and fibre such as straw) and even as a mortar for stone construction. Rammed earth has been used for centuries, and is perhaps most famously used in Shibam in Yemen and Ait-Ben-Haddou in Morocco. Perhaps more surprising are the large numbers of rammed earth houses and barns in central and northern France and across the UK. One of the great benefits of rammed earth is that it is necessarily local, so your architecture can be literally built of the ground it stands on.

Rowland Keable describes himself as a builder, but he is also a lecturer, the UNESCO Chair of Earthen Architecture, and a great advocate of rammed earth construction. Importantly, alongside his built projects he has been instrumental in drawing up design codes and training guides for the use of rammed earth. As a builder, Keable explains the importance of the initial site survey, and that as much as possible you want to use the material you have on site. This is one of the many environmental benefits of this type of construction – it removes the need for unnecessary transportation of heavy building materials. On a large-scale construction, Keable will collect material on site and make initial samples for structural testing, alongside the analysis of clay and moisture content, which is critical for successful binding of the materials. Earth and chalk can be used in rammed earth construction, but it is important that this does not include topsoil that contains organic material. The material is mixed on site, either by hand or mechanically, and then is placed into a formwork like that used for in-situ cast concrete and filled with layers of lose soil. The soil is then compacted as layers, either by hand 'rams' or mechanically with pneumatic 'tampers' until the section wall is complete. One of the big differences between a rammed earth and a concrete wall is that you can remove or 'strike' the formwork as soon as you have completed the compacting process, with no curing time required.

↑ **Fig 3.03.1** Brighton Waste House and a rammed chalk wall under construction. Rammed Earth Consulting.

← **Fig 3.03.2** Construction of curved rammed chalk walls using adapted formwork usually employed for in-situ cast concrete, Pines Calyx, Brighton. Rammed Earth Consulting.

Rammed earth walls are typically unreinforced, so they tend to be at least 300 mm thick. Rammed earth walls are also thermally massive, and help to regulate the internal temperature and humidity levels within a building as they can absorb and re-radiate excess heat and coolth. Keable's method integrates with more standard contemporary construction technology by building off a concrete floor slab and using a slim layer of reinforced concrete at intermediate floor levels to provide localised support and fixing for steel or timber floor beams. However, he is adamant in not using cement in the rammed earth mix (referred to as 'stabilised earth' and preventing total recyclability), which is another of its great benefits.

3.04 Fabric Formwork: Minishell

Designer: Dante Bini

'The main characteristics of this technique is that the concrete is poured on a membrane in [a] flat position on the ground and is then lifted and shaped by inflating the membrane.'[44]

– Dante Bini

While Dante Bini was a student of architecture he was inspired by the thin concrete shells of Adalberto Libera and Pier Luigi Nervi. However, he also observed that the timber formwork used in the making of these structures cost more in time and materials than the structure itself, only to be discarded after a single use. In 1964, Bini successfully constructed in three hours a 12 m diameter, 6 m high hemispherical reinforced concrete shell structure using his unique pneumatic formwork of a giant fabric balloon.

↑ **Fig 3.04.1** Construction of a Minishell showing a newly formed shell in the foreground, Dante Bini and Jennings Ind., NSW, Australia, 1980.

↑ **Fig 3.04.2** Minishell foundations in the foreground with Bini's stretched steel 'spring' reinforcement system, Dante Bini and Jennings Ind., NSW, Australia, 1980.

↑ **Fig 3.04.3** A Minishell during the inflation process, Dante Bini and Jennings Ind., NSW, Australia, 1980.

The Minishell construction system is a development of his original Binishell patent, which used an inflatable fabric formwork to lift and shape wet concrete into a thin reinforced concrete shell. Minishell is designed to produce small, 8 x 8 m (maximum 10 x 10 m) low-cost, square or octagonal, monolithic reinforced concrete shell structures, provided with openings at the corners which result from the construction process. Bini had observed the difficulties of manoeuvring, positioning, anchoring and folding the inflatable membrane, especially in his larger 36 m diameter Binishell domes). These largest membranes had a surface area of 1,000 m² and could weigh over 1500 kg. The 8 x 8 m Minishell system is designed to use less than 5 m³ of concrete for the structural shell and can be formed (excluding site preparation and foundations) in only 30 minutes. This equates to 1.5 labour hours per m² of covered area. Interestingly, the protruding upturned edges formed around the corner openings during inflation help to create a raised 'lip', which acts to stiffen the openings. Several tourist villages in both Australia and Italy were built using the Minishell system. In Trinity Beach, Cairns in Queensland, Bini designed and oversaw the construction of a holiday village that was completed in 1978. An 8 x 8 m Minishell requires 4.6 m³ of concrete, reinforced with 400 (6 mm diameter) steel reinforcement rods and 200 (36 mm outer diameter, 2 mm thick) hard-drawn wire springs.

The square plan (parallel edges) enables quick installation of the foundation system, and the speed of construction and material economy of the Minishell have led to a recent re-evaluation of the system by Bini and his architect son Nicoló. They have explored how the Minishell technology might be successfully deployed in disaster relief and reconstruction schemes for low-cost housing, food stores and clinics. They are quick to build, strong, fireproof and with an extremely economical and sustainable use of cementitious material. With the more recent development of fibre-reinforced cementious products, the steel reinforcement of the original Minishell could be replaced, but the imperative of the original Binishell remains: eliminating wasteful and costly timber shuttering with reusable inflatable formwork.

3.05 Pneumatic Structures: Desert Cloud

Designer: Graham Stevens

'Desert Cloud was a move away from the singular notion of shelter as a protection against the outside, towards a new conception of shelter in which you experience the atmosphere, the environment.' [45]

– Graham Stevens

Graham Stevens pioneered the development and use of pneumatic structures during an explosion of interest in the promise of 'inflatable' architecture across Europe and the US in the late 1960s and early 1970s. Stevens had studied as an architect under professor J.K. Page, author of Note 50 of the World Meteorological Organization (WMO) report 'Climate in Towns' (1959), stating that 'Buildings articulate climate'. In 1967 Stevens attended the first International Colloquium on Pneumatic Structures (organised by the International Association for Shell Structures, IASS) at the University of Stuttgart. The colloquium (chaired by Frei Otto) hosted the leaders of this rapidly evolving technological art, including Walter Bird, Victor Lundy, Nikolaus Laing and Cedric Price. Stevens created large-scale inflatable sculptures such as his Transmobile works, which featured at countercultural festivals, and he subsequently developed the Atmosfield works, which included his 'walking on water' tubes, and ultimately his emblematic Desert Cloud project of 1974.

Desert Cloud was produced for a film of the same name that Stevens made, documenting the history of the relationship between architecture and the sun following the oil crisis of 1973. Desert Cloud works by absorbing solar energy through the transparent membrane on the top, and this high-frequency radiation is converted to low-frequency radiation (light to heat) by internal black membrane structural webs, in a process reinforced by reflectance from the lower surface of silver fabric. This specific arrangement captures the radiation of the sun through the transparent layer, and shortens the wavelength with the black internal panels, heating the air inside. The heated air expands, which inflates the structure, and the rising heat creates buoyancy and finally lifts the structure. The reflective underside provides much-needed desert shade. Desert Cloud requires no electricity and contains no moving parts, and with solar energy arriving every day the main problem is how best to 'tune into' that source. Stevens also demonstrated how the structure could capture and condense water on its surface, even in the desert. He explained in a lecture that the problem with accepting new ideas in relation to energy harnessing is not to do with technical solutions, but rather '... it's about a change in perception and art is about changes in perception'. Desert Cloud was

'... a move away from the singular notion of shelter as a protection against the outside, and a new conception of shelter in which you experience the atmosphere, the environment'. [46]

↑ **Fig 3.05.1** Self-buoyant Desert Cloud sculpture by Graham Stevens, Arabian Desert. Still from the film 'Desert Cloud' (1974).

↑ Fig 3.05.2 400 m long 'Wavetube', Cornwall by Graham Stevens. Still of 'Wavetube' (1971) from the film 'Atmosfields' (1968-71).

↑ Fig 3.05.3 Graham Stevens 'walking on water'.
Still of 'Pontube' (1970) for 'Locations Edinburgh' (1971).

3.06	**Steel Monocoque Construction: The Neuron Pod**
	Designer: Will Alsop – aLL Design and AKT II

'Monocoque literally means "single shell", and simply describes the "purest" approach to surface structures - the sole use of a thin surface without any stiffening ribs. Combinations of surface and ribs are "semi-monocoques", also referred to as stressed-skin.'[47]

– Martin Bechthold

A monocoque or semi-monocoque structure is defined in the automotive industry as the integration of the chassis and body as a single structure. In construction, we can describe a monocoque as the merging of structural frame and skin into a single 'structural skin', where the geometric form of the surface itself provides its strength. Monocoque or stressed-skin construction is more typically used in the nautical, aeronautical and car industries, where reducing weight has been seen as a more critical design imperative. However, the increased focus in the construction industry on embedded energy, material resource and structural redundancy would suggest a re-evaluation of design prerogatives and a renewed emphasis on lightness and material efficiency.

The award-winning biomedical research building for Queen Mary University known as the Blizard Building (completed in 2005) was designed by Will Alsop and contains four large cell-inspired suspended pod-like structures. Alsop was subsequently invited to add a fifth 'pod' that would sit outside the main buildings in Blizard Mews, which was to be his last building. The Neuron Pod is constructed of 13 prefabricated steel sections, which each weigh between 1.5 and 7.7 tonnes. The prefabricated sections were made at Littlehampton Welding and then craned into position, before being bolted and welded together on site to provide a weatherproof exterior. The Neuron Pod sits above Blizard's underground research laboratories, and so the structure was designed to distribute weight on to the back legs (supported by the basement retaining wall) and the single front leg, which is aligned with a basement column. The monocoque construction of the pod allowed for the structural optimisation of this zoomorphic beastie, with the total weight of the building kept to 41 tonnes (with a 25 tonne steel structure). The 25 tonnes equated to the weight of the truck that delivered each of the steel components.

The Neuron Pod is fabricated from 12 m long segmental strips of 8 mm Corten®[48] steel, plasma-cut and roll-formed. The steel segments were then welded to internal ribs to stiffen the skin. The structure is thermally insulated with a sprayed expanding foam insulation. Following installation, a steel truss bridge was slid into the mouth of the pod, forming a connection with the main building. The pod provides an 84 m² meeting space and is covered with 500 fibre-optic 'dendrites' on the exterior that light up at night.

↑ **Fig 3.06.1** Cor-ten® steel Neuron Pod, with colour-changing fibre-optic 'hairs', Queen Mary's University, London.

← **Fig 3.06.2** Interior of the Neuron Pod during assembly of the prefabricated sections.

↓ **Fig 3.06.3** Drawing showing the structural ribs and connection with the existing bridge.

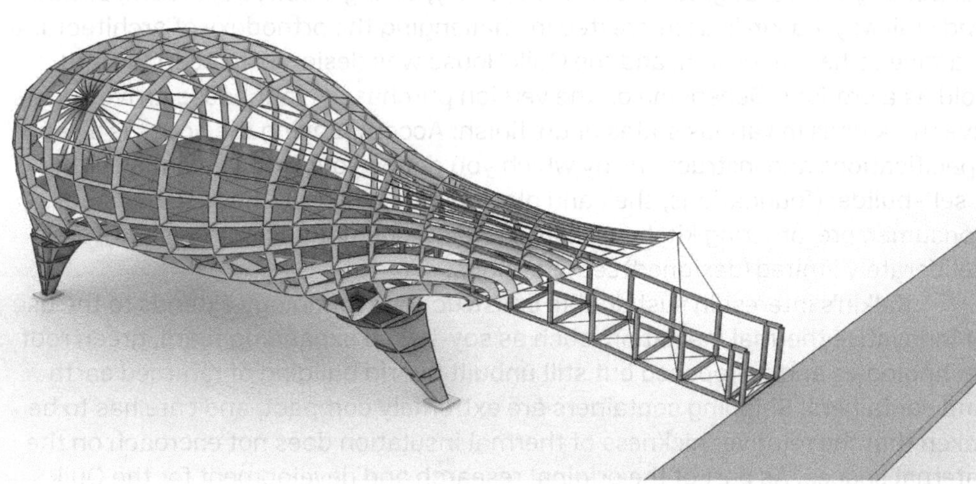

3.07	**Upcycled Shipping Containers: Quik House**
	Designer: Adam Kalkin

'... the natural laws of conservation of energy and our own perpetual industriousness force us to look at our garbage with fresh eyes. We either break it down into a more elemental, usable form or we repurpose it.'[49]

– Adam Kalkin

The architecture of Adam Kalkin has often involved the useful appropriation of technology, such as his set-piece Bunny Lane house, which cocoons a 19th-century rural New Jersey clapboard cottage in a portal-frame steel shed. In 2001 Kalkin began working with shipping containers as modular units for his designs, and he launched a prototype of his Quik House (a 200 m² family dwelling) in the Deitch Gallery, New York City in 2004. Kalkin is keen to stress that the imperative for the Quik House and building with shipping containers does not come from architecture, more that it is made possible by container surpluses created by imbalances in global trade.

The shipping container was brought to market by Malcolm McLean, and McLean's containers were first unloaded in Newark, New Jersey in 1956. In Kalkin's appropriate New Jersey base he oversees the customisation and repurposing of the standardised volume of an ISO shipping container. The design, fabrication and material specification of the ISO container is high quality and ubiquitous and so, even when using out-of-service containers, you are generally working with structurally sound units. In the Quik House, Kalkin cleverly challenges the boxy modularity of the container, using its spanning potential to a create a large ground floor kitchen and living space. Kalkin also skillfully populates the small supporting 'cubes' at ground level with pantry, dining 'nook', boot room, bathroom and stairway. Kalkin is as interested in challenging the orthodoxy of architectural practice as he is in design, and the Quik House was designed to be made and sold as a product. Depending on the version purchased, your house arrives in five truckloads in various states of un-finish. Accompanying the house is a set of specifications and instructions by which you define your involvement as either a self-builder (foundations, shell and glazing only) or a fully-fledged housing consumer, pre-ordering kitchens, exterior paint colour and floor finishes from a deliberately limited (designed) set of options.

Kalkin's interest in sustainable construction technology extends to the use of innovative thermal insulation, such as soy-based expanding foam, green roof technologies and a proposed but still unbuilt hybrid building of rammed earth and containers. Shipping containers are extremely compact, and care has to be taken that the relative thickness of thermal insulation does not encroach on the internal spaces. As part of the original research and development for the Quik

House, Kalkin investigated the use of aerogel blanket as thermal insulation. This super-thin blanket, originally developed for industrial applications, is now being used in construction, in particular for restoration projects where improved thermal performance must be incorporated within tight physical confines. Other key projects by Kalkin include the Adriance House, a large residence in Maine in which bedrooms, bathrooms and other discrete spaces are all housed within shipping containers and then wrapped in a larger shed, and his emblematic Pushbutton House, which mechanises a single container with hydraulic actuators, opening doors and walls and transforming into a single micro-home at the push of a button.

↑ **Fig 3.07.1** Original Quik House marketing brochure, Adam Kalkin, 2004.

↑ **Fig 3.07.2** Assembly of a Quik House by Adam Kalkin, Califon, New Jersey, 2007.

↗ **Fig 3.07.3** Completed Quik House and neighbouring Old Lady House by Adam Kalkin, Califon, New Jersey, 2007.

→ **Fig 3.07.4** Completed Quik House by Adam Kalkin, Califon, New Jersey, 2007. Kalkin has left the original paintwork of the 'Triton' containers.

TRITON
TRITON
TRITON

3.08	**Tensegrity Structures: Tension Pavilion**
	Designers: StructureMode and Weber Industries

'… "Tensegrity" icosahedra give the most environmental enclosure per pound (weight) and volume of material employed.'[50]

– Richard Buckminster Fuller

Richard Buckminster Fuller coined the word tensegrity, which was formed from 'tension' and 'integrity', as one of his composite designed nouns; it was first included in *The Oxford English Dictionary* in 1985. The tensegrity structure itself was jointly invented by Richard Buckminster Fuller and artist Kenneth Snelson. Snelson was a student of Fuller's at Black Mountain College, North Carolina, USA, and over two summers from 1948 to 1949 he formalised the structural invention of the tensegrity structure, which he called 'continuous tension, discontinuous compression structures'. In keeping with Fuller's doctrine of doing more with less the tensegrity principle makes optimal structural use of material properties by clearly separating compressive elements (struts), which are simultaneously held together and apart within a tensile wire matrix. The resultant structures remove structural redundancy and are incredibly material efficient, without the need for the large ground anchors required by a more conventional tensile structure.

The tensegrity Tension Pavilion by Geoff Morrow's StructureMode is a continuous toroidal structure formed of three arches, and comprises 24 interconnected tensegrity modules supported at three points. The torus tensegrity 'edge beam' is designed to support an anticlastic tensile fabric canopy in the centre. The three base connections are created with hexagonal steel hoops, which effectively hold the tensegrity structure in suspension. The compressive struts are formed from softwood timber and machined into double-ended 'pencil-like' members, with a metal boss embedded in each end, and a detachable D-shackle that can attach multiple pre-cut and measured wire-rope cables.

The cell biologist and founding director of the Wyss Institute for Biologically Inspired Engineering at Harvard University, Don E. Ingber, has written about tensegrity structures, and what he sees as the connection between living cells: 'An astoundingly wide variety of natural systems, including carbon atoms, water molecules, proteins, viruses, cells, tissues and even humans and other living creatures are constructed using a common form of architecture known as tensegrity … tensegrity structures are mechanically stable not because of the strength of individual members, but because of the way the entire structure distributes and balances mechanical stresses.'[51] And while this structural type is a rarely seen commodity, its inherent strength and lightness offer huge possibilities in the fields of architecture and construction.

↑ **Fig 3.08.1** Assembly of StructureMode's Tension Pavilion by architecture students from the University of Westminster, 2016.

↑ **Fig 3.08.2** Detail of StructureMode's Tension Pavilion, showing the timber 'pencil' struts, 2016.

↑ **Fig 3.08.3** StructureMode's Tension Pavilion, University of Westminster, 2016.

3.09	**Timber Gridshell: Mannheim Multihalle**
	Designers: Frei Otto, Carlfried Mutschler and Joachim Langner, with engineers Ted Happold and Ian Liddell (Restoration Fast + Epp)

'The ratio of the thickness of the (grid) shell to the span is approximately .00625. In comparison, the ratio of thickness to mean diameter of an average eggshell is .007, indicating that the Mannheim Multihalle is proportionately thinner than an eggshell!'[52]

– Jarred Mihalik, et al.

In 1971 architects Carlfried Mutschler and Joachim Langner won the competition to build a multipurpose hall to host a biennial horticultural exhibition in Mannheim. They engaged the help of Frei Otto and his Atelier Warmbronn, and the multifunctional hall was completed in 1974. Over 40 years later, in 2016, this 'temporary' building with a design life of only two years was scheduled for demolition. The outcry that followed has saved this much-loved icon of Mannheim (now a historical monument), and the building is currently undergoing refurbishment and restoration by the Canadian practice Fast + Epp.

This unique timber gridshell (or lattice shell) roof structure remains the largest self-supporting timber gridshell in the world, with roof spans of more than 80 m and rising to almost 19 m at its highest point. Hemlock 50 x 50 mm timber laths are alternately laid across each other (four members thick) on an even 500 x 500 mm grid. Where the members intersect, a bolt connects them at each nodal point, with slots cut in the outer timber members to allow for movement. The timber grid is assembled flat on the ground and is then lifted in sections by scaffolding towers and a forklift truck. When a section has reached its required height, the bolts are tightened and the edge fixed to a beam that locks the structure in place. A crisscrossing grid of cables runs over the structure (at every sixth node), which helps to resist buckling in wind or snowy conditions. The timber gridshell is then wrapped in a translucent fabric membrane. The completed gridshell (7400 m^2) acts in compression to efficiently carry vertical loads, with the strength of such a thin structure derived from its doubly curved geometry.

The design of the gridshell was developed with the help of Frei Otto's 'form-finding' model technique in addition to numerical analysis. A 1:500 suspended chain model of the structure was created, with a grid of wire cables covering the surface area of the model. The cables represented the wooden lathes that would form the gridshell in the final structure. The suspended cable-net worked as a good model for the Mannheim Multihalle, because it was put under tensile forces from its self-weight.

Other significant lightweight gridshell structures are the Weald and Downland Museum by Ted Cullinan and Ted Happold (Buro Happold), which was made with green oak lathes, and the Hanover Expo Japan Pavilion (2000) by Shigeru Ban, Buro Happold and Frei Otto, where the timber was replaced with cardboard tubes.

↑ Fig 3.09.1 Mannheim timber gridshell, by Frei Otto, Carlfried Mutschler and Joachim Langner, with engineers Ted Happold and Ian Liddell, 1975.

→ Fig 3.09.2 Interior of the timber gridshell structure showing the overlaid timber lathes clamped at joints. Weald and Downland Open Air Museum, Singleton. Edward Cullinan Architects, 2001.

3.10 Cross-Laminated Timber

Designer: Waugh Thistleton Architects

'A mass timber building will weigh about 30% of a regular building, and so much reduced foundations ... these buildings can be re-purposed, they are easy to adapt.' [53]

– Andrew Waugh

CLT is an engineered timber product with great structural properties and a low carbon footprint. It is a panelised product made from small kiln-dried and finger-jointed timber planks (between 20 mm and 45 mm thick) layered in right-angle (90°) laminations. Each layer is sprayed with a PVA or PUR adhesive and then clamped together under a huge press. CLT is made up of a minimum of three layers (60 mm) up to a maximum sheet thickness of 500 mm. The wood species typically used are softwood spruce, pine, fir and larch. There is no theoretical limit to the sheet size, but transportation limitations will normally restrict panel sizes to a maximum length of 16.5 m, and width of 3 m. One of the benefits of CLT is its prefabrication, which allows for precise factory cutting and routing of the material for openings and services, minimising site work and thus reducing waste and improving build quality. The structural integrity of CLT panels means that openings for windows and doors do not require additional structures such as lintels, and the 'mass' nature of this solid timber substrate provides for great surface fixing throughout the structure as well as a measure of thermal and acoustic insulation.

CLT panels provide a good level of thermal insulation and avoid thermal bridging, but depending on the wall thickness will usually require an additional layer of insulation. The insulation of a CLT building usually happens externally, with an additional rain-screen protection. This allows the inside finish to be CLT, which is effective for moderating internal climate. CLT buildings have been clad in timber, composite panels, render and brick cavity wall construction. As it uses renewably sourced timber, CLT has a low embodied carbon content, with carbon sequestered and stored through tree growth.

Andrew Waugh of Waugh Thistleton Architects is a great advocate for CLT, and he first used it in a small project in 2003. His practice subsequently built a nine-storey residential CLT tower in Murray Grove, Hackney, London and has demonstrated its success in the construction of dense urban housing projects. Waugh has also used newer engineered timber products such as LVL, which is a large section of bonded timber veneers providing the equivalent cross-sectional strength of steel.

↑ **Fig 3.10.1** Cutaway drawing showing how CLT is used as floors and balconies in a hybrid structure with lightweight perforated steel beams. Orsman Road, London. Waugh Thistleton Architects, 2020.

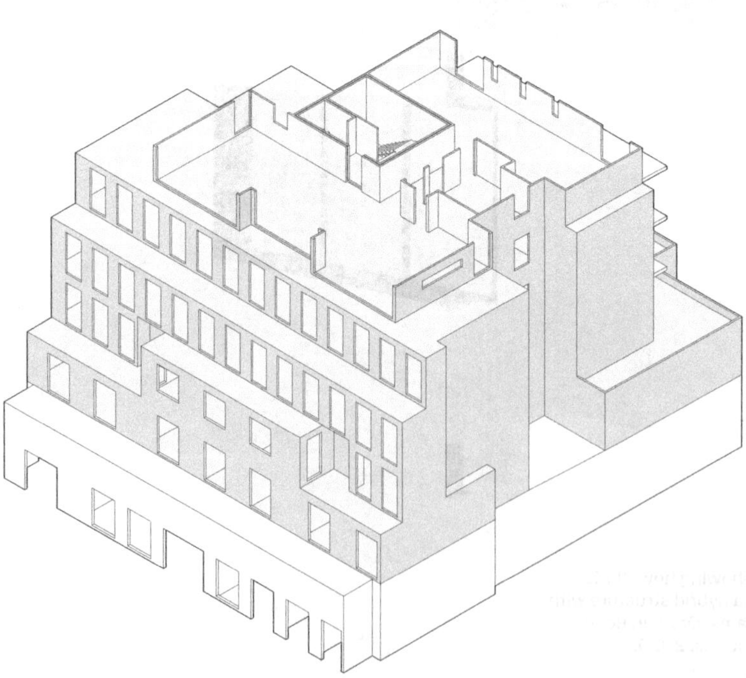

ISOMETRIC SECTIONAL DRAWING

↖ **Fig 3.10.2** Orsman Road project during construction, showing CLT floor slabs and CLT upstand with steel frame. Waugh Thistleton Architects, 2020. Tim Crocker.

← **Fig 3.10.3** Pitfield Street cinema and housing; yellow indicates structural CLT panels. Waugh Thistleton Architects, 2020.

↑ **Fig 3.10.4** Pitfield Street cinema and housing during construction showing CLT floor slabs, glulam columns and steel beams. Waugh Thistleton Architects, 2020. Lewis Khan.

‘Pollution is nothing but resources we’re not harvesting. We allow them to disperse because we’ve been ignorant of their value.’[54]

Richard Buckminster Fuller

Chapter 4
Heating, Cooling and Remediation

The relative movement of heat energy remains critical for our human comfort. The remediation in the title of this chapter refers to the harvesting of pollution and its successful metabolic transformation from hazardous pollutant to benign compound or sequestered substrate. The recent shift in emphasis from energy 'in use' to the 'embodied' energy of construction should not distract us from the importance of how we can sustainably heat and cool (and clean) our built environment. Vernacular construction has much to teach us about local climatic adaptation, material use and built form; in Rosa Schiano-Phan's research on evaporative cooling she identifies how the porosity of clay can be employed for passive cooling in hot and dry climates, and how the rediscovery of this ancient technology is both relevant and timely.

John Todd's Eco-Machines® are like a biological 'soup' whose recipe can be designed to filter out and clean polluted land and water, and that Todd remains so optimistic about the power of his 'machines' to remediate poisoned earth and water is heartening. In the 'smog-eating facade' of a Mexican hospital, designers Allison Dring and Daniel Schwaag maximise the surface area of an elaborate scrim of material that wraps a building (appropriately, a hospital) in a new kind of interstitial layer that cleans the air. It does this by metabolising the nitrogen oxide (NOx) of vehicle exhaust fumes through a photocatalytic process powered by the sun. In Rosa Schiano-Phan's research on evaporative cooling she identifies how the porosity of clay can be employed for passive cooling in hot and dry climates, and how the rediscovery of this ancient technology is both relevant and timely. The air source heat pump (ASHP) of Bunhill 2 Energy Centre is ingenious in its location – the ventilation chimney of an underground railway tunnel – with the heat-exchange process used to capture waste heat and redeploy that energy to heat local housing. Likewise, the ground source heat pump (GSHP) technology incorporated into the structural foundations of a new building is a brilliant piece of systems thinking that moves 'waste' heat energy to where it is required, and uses the thermal mass of concrete pile foundations to store it. The Rjukan Sun Mirrors could be seen as an expensive novelty, but this project by local artist Martin Anderson realised the 100-year-old dream of local industrialist Sam Eyde to bring sun into the overshadowed Norweigan town of Rjukan, and provide visual pleasure as well as much-needed vitamin D. Steve and Holly Baer's Zome House remains an iconic environmental building, in which they use walls of stacked water-filled steel drums to store and release heat energy in the desert climate of New Mexico. A more detailed study of this project also shows how the building includes earth walls for thermal mass and insulated shutters as part of a sophisticated but technically simple climatic control system. The Baers have dedicated their professional lives to the development, promotion and sales of passive solar technology. In Atelier Ten's Thermal Labyrinth, the principles of thermal storage are employed with the heavy mass of concrete used for energy storage and release. The process is brilliantly managed via a subterranean (and labyrinthine) maze of concrete, cleverly crenellated for improved transference of heat. Harold Hay's Roofpond replaces the heat storage potential of concrete with water, which has excellent heat storage and release properties, and adds a movable layer of thermal insulation so that excess heat can be purged into the cool night sky of Arizona. Finally, the wind catchers or *badgir* of Yazd in Iran are described. These sophisticated passive cooling systems are highly effective at mitigating the extremely high air temperatures of central Iran. They provide an object lesson in achieving human comfort through skillful design and construction, and their integration into the fabric and form of the architecture.

This book does not explicitly feature energy generation technology such as wind turbines, photovoltaics, biomass or hydroelectric, and while these low-carbon technologies are not excluded from the designer's palette, it might be that their relative success is better achieved at larger scale. The technology of thermal mass and thermal insulation is simple, but its application need not be; likewise, the technology of heat pumps is well understood and not new, but its application in projects like Bunhill 2 in London creates new possibilities for the interconnectedness of buildings and infrastructure, and their relative and potentially shared use of heat energy.

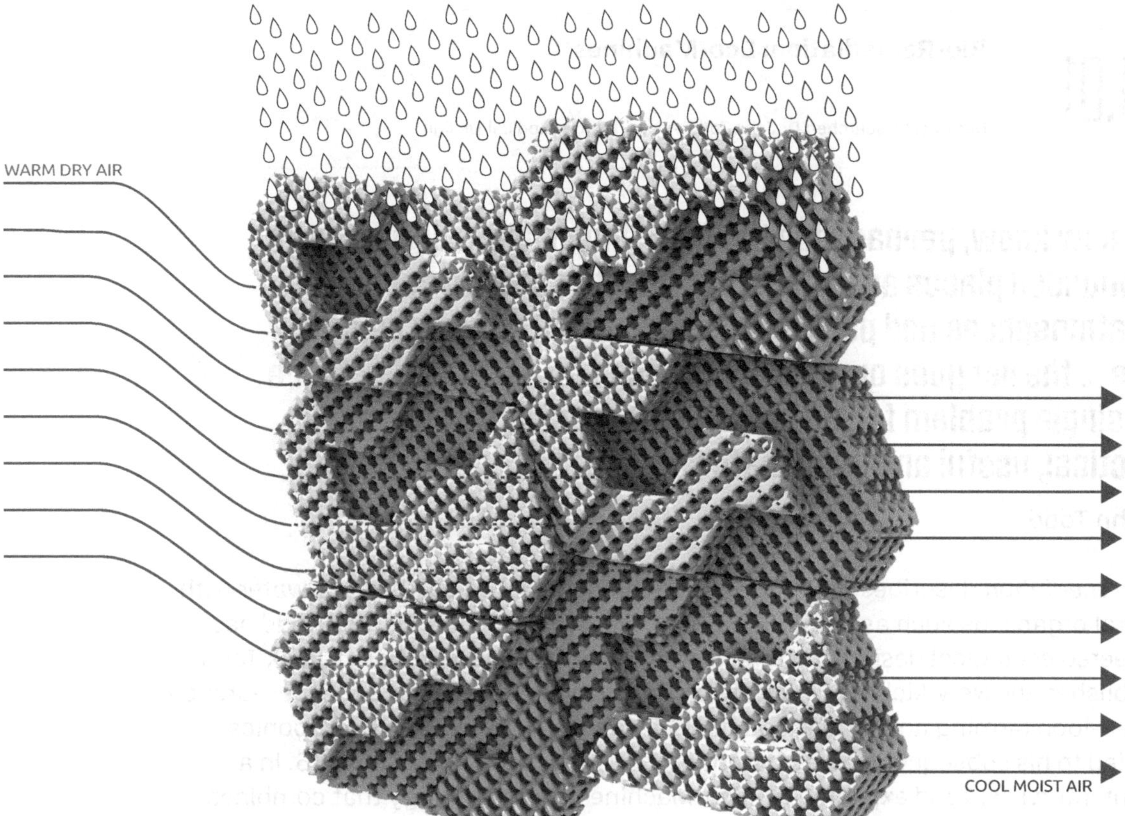

↑ **Fig 4.00.1** Diagram showing how the 3D printed porous ceramic 'Cool Brick' cools warm air through an evaporative cooling process by Emerging Objects.

4.01	**Bio-Remediation: Eco-Machines®**
	Designer/Researcher: Dr John Todd – John Todd Ecological Design

'We now know, perhaps for the first time in history, how to go to wounded places and heal them; how to stabilize carbon in the atmosphere and park it (or sequester) it into the earth's soils ... the list goes on. Of what we can't do, I don't think there is a single problem facing humanity for which there is not a practical, useful and immediate solution.'[55]

– John Todd

Bio-remediation describes the process of cleaning polluted earth, air or water with natural organisms such as bacteria or fungi. For over 30 years Dr John Todd has pioneered ecological design and engineering. Todd and his wife Nancy Jack Todd established the New Alchemy Institute on Cape Cod in 1969, where they researched closed-loop farming and food production. It was Todd's work with hydroponics that led to his subsequent development of the first Eco-Machine® in 1986. In a recent interview, Todd explains: 'An Eco-Machine® is a technology that combines civil engineering and ecological life. They can be designed to grow foods, they can be designed to treat waste, they can be designed to purify water, they can be designed to repair damaged environments ... and in some instances, they can be designed to also provide fuels.'[56] The Eco-Machine® is less mechanically complex than its name might suggest, and the custom design of each 'machine' consists of a series of tanks and ponds and growing substrates and environments that contain all of the five (or six) kingdoms of life, which might include microscopic algae, fungi, bacteria, protozoa, snails, fish and zooplankton. Through biomimicry (inspired by nature and natural systems), Todd has been able to deliver bespoke systems that have been used for the removal of industrial waste such as oils and other toxic contaminants from water courses, as well as to create sewage and waste treatment plants. Todd has delivered successful projects all over the world, working with local municipal authorities and businesses to clean, rehabilitate and remediate polluted water using natural systems inspired by and learned from nature. The Eco-Machine® is a complex – but importantly, visible – system that also successfully functions as learning and teaching environments for schools and universities. Todd explains that '... all an ecological designer is, is someone who uses the strategies of an eco-system like a lake or a pond, or a marsh or a salt-marsh, or a wood, to carry out the work of society'.[57]

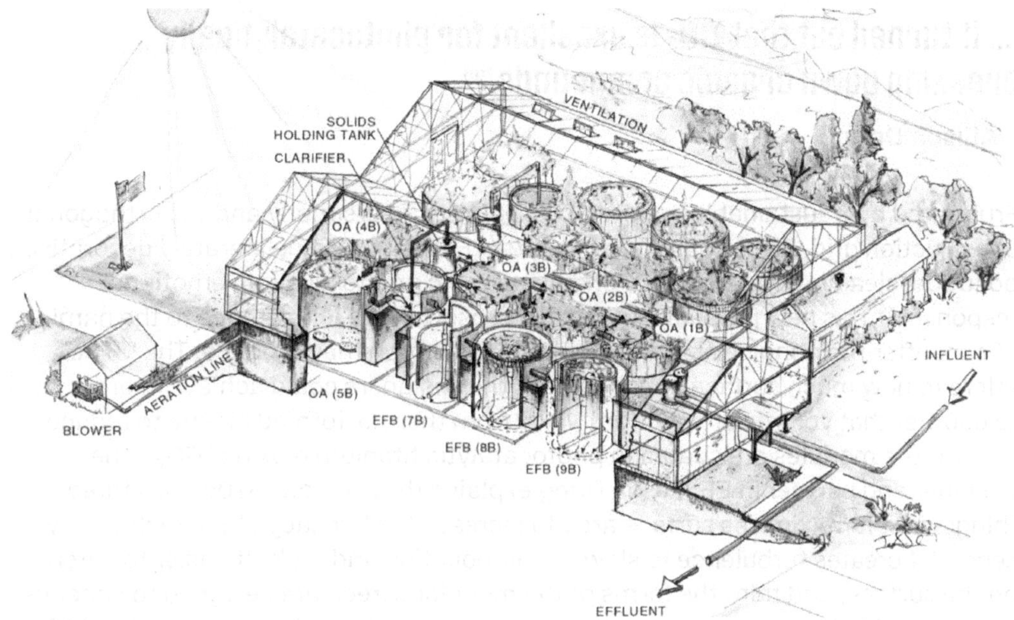

↑ **Fig 4.01.1** Diagram of Eco-Machine® for City of South Burlington municipal installation.

4.02	**Bio-Remediation: Smog-Eating Facade**
	Location: Hospital Manuel Gea González, Tlalpan, Mexico City
	Designers: Allison Dring and Daniel Schwaag – Elegant Embellishments

'… it turned out that TiO_2 is excellent for photocatalytically breaking down organic compounds.'[58]

– Allison Dring

Frustrated by a sustainable architectural palette of parsimony and the orthogonal construction grid, Elegant Embellishments (EE) designed a deliberately decorative pollution-cleaning screen, based on an aperiodic grid to 'elicit an emotional response'.[59] This new product was named prosolve370e in reference to the naming of cars after their engine size and how much pollution they produce. The '370e' refers to how much surface enhancement the designers could achieve in order to counter that volume of pollution. Made from thermo-formed plastic to reduce weight, the modules are coated in photocatalytic titanium dioxide (TiO_2). The designer and partner in EE Allison Dring explains that prosolve370e does three things: first it maximises surface area to increase the 'efficacy of the technology'; second it creates turbulence to slow the air pollution and make it easier to catch on the surface; and third the forms of the modular screen are designed to enhance reception of light, including the reflected light of neighbouring modules. In 2012, the technology was installed at the Hospital Manuel Gea González in Mexico City, described as 'the incredible smog-eating building'[60] by CNN.

The screen covers an area of 25,000 m² and is thought to be the world's largest engineered urban air-purifier. Based on the size of the screen, and its maximised surface area, EE claims to achieve around 5000 m² of photocatalytic activity, which equates to mitigating the air pollution produced by 1,000 cars per day. Air pollution is composed of two key ingredients: oxides of nitrogen (known as NOx) and volatile organic compounds (VOCs), which are both produced by combustion engines.

The screen is coated in a superfine 'nano' layer of TiO_2, a compound more commonly used as a white pigment and toothpaste additive; its photocatalytic properties are activated by sunlight to reduce air pollution. The photocatalytic process works when the surface receives photons of light from solar energy (even on an overcast day), and when noxious NOx and VOCs come into contact with the TiO_2 substrate they are broken down by a chemical 'redox' reaction, which yields calcium nitrate (useful as a fertiliser), washed off the surface by rain.

↑ Fig 4.02.1 Hospital Manuel Gea González, with the detail of the 'smog-eating facade', Mexico City, 2012. Elegant Embellishments.

← Fig 4.02.2 The form of the facade screen is designed to maximise the surface area and contact with the polluted air. Elegant Embellishments.

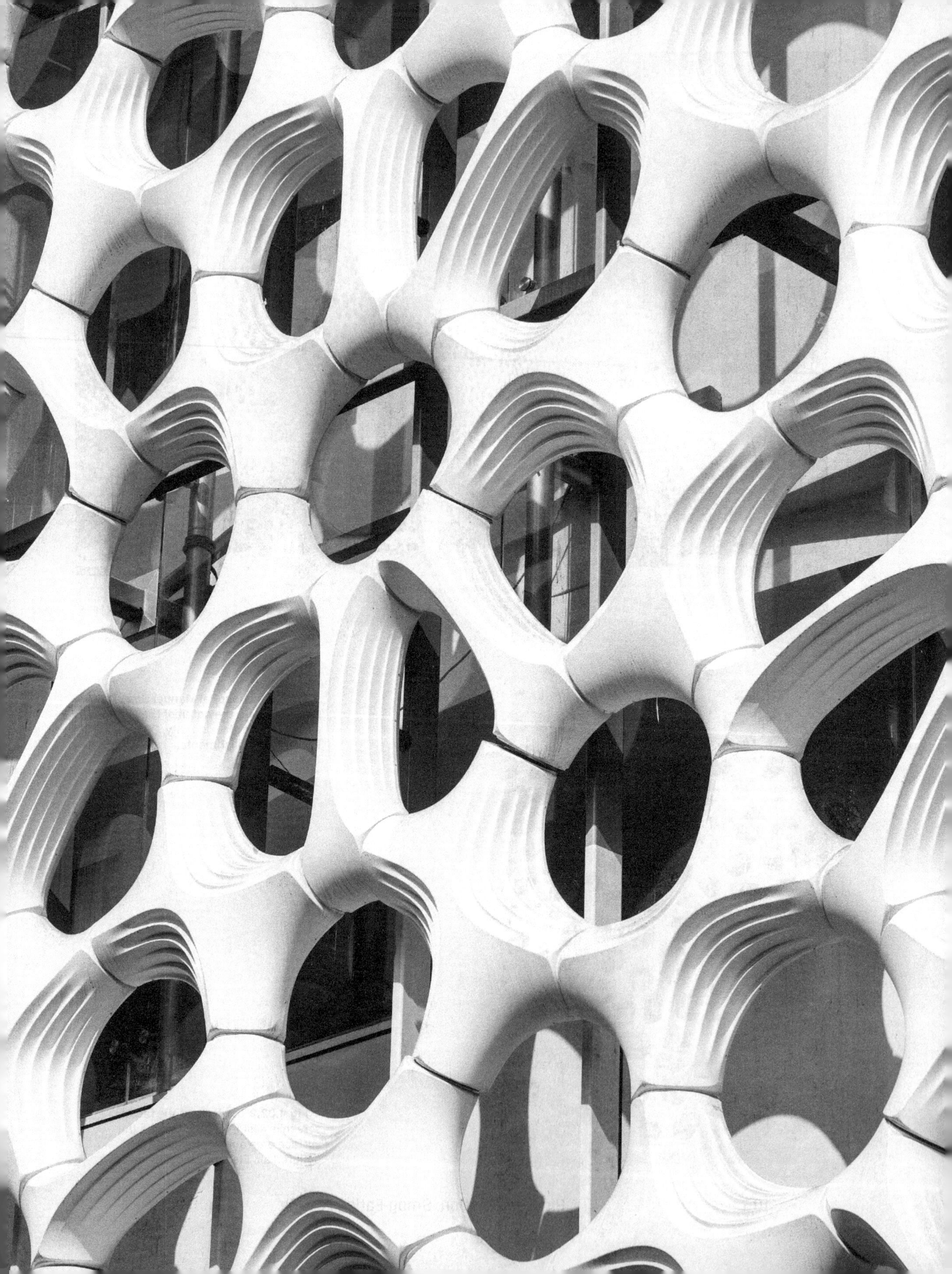

↑ **Fig 4.02.4** View from inside the hospital, which shows how the photocatalytic modular elements are bolted together. Elegant Embellishments.

← **Fig 4.02.3** The facade screen also provides solar shade. Elegant Embellishments.

4.03	Evaporative Cooling
	Designer/Researcher: Rosa Schiano-Phan

'An "innovative" passive evaporative cooling system using porous ceramic components can be integrated in residential buildings. This can meet the cooling loads of existing housing apartments.'[61]

– Rosa Schiano-Phan

Evaporative cooling is the cooling effect stimulated by the adiabatic evaporation of water. When humans perspire and our sweat dries, this local evaporation acts to cool our body. The unglazed clay of a terracotta pot enables this process through its material porosity, which will allow water to saturate the clay. As this water reaches the outer surface of the pot, evaporation occurs (depending on the exterior temperature), causing a cooling effect on the liquid inside. This centuries-old process cools water by as much as 12–15°C below ambient temperatures.

A traditional window system from Muscat in Oman incorporates a large water-filled terracotta pot as part of a projecting window. These self-shading and finely louvred window openings prevent sun entering the room, allow hot air to escape, and will cool incoming air with evaporative cooling while still providing a view from inside. The wind-catcher towers of Iran and Iraq have historically incorporated water-filled ceramic vessels, and a variation of this technology (the *maziara* water jar) has also been used in Egypt in combination with wind-catcher towers to improve their cooling performance.

A more recent development of this principle was explored in the EvapCool research project (Schiano-Phan, et al.). This system comprises a series of interlocking slip-cast hollow clay blocks that are filled with water. The idea is to integrate these panels into the perimeter walls of office developments. Initial assessment of the technology is promising, but it does require a large surface area to be effective. In a second residential case study in Seville, Spain, the technology proved successful in a retrofit residential building. In a later iteration, the designers have developed Cool-wall, which introduces surface texture and patterning on to the ceramic, increasing the surface area and thus improving its cooling potential. Another recent example of ceramic evaporative technology is the Ecooler by Studio Khan, which has reinterpreted a traditional *mashrabiya* screen as a filigree water-filled ceramic 'cooling' surface. New digital fabrication techniques have also led to the creation of Cool Brick by 3D-printing gurus Emerging Objects. The Cool Brick is a 3D-printed porous ceramic brick, which absorbs water like a sponge; as air passes through a wall of these bricks it is evaporatively cooled. Additionally, the unique shape of the brick helps to self-shade the outer surface of the wall to keep it cool and protected from the sun, which improves performance.

Evaporative cooling with porous ceramic and water works in hot and dry climates, as well as temperate climates with a dry season or at dry times, but it will not work in a hot and humid environment where the air is already saturated with water.

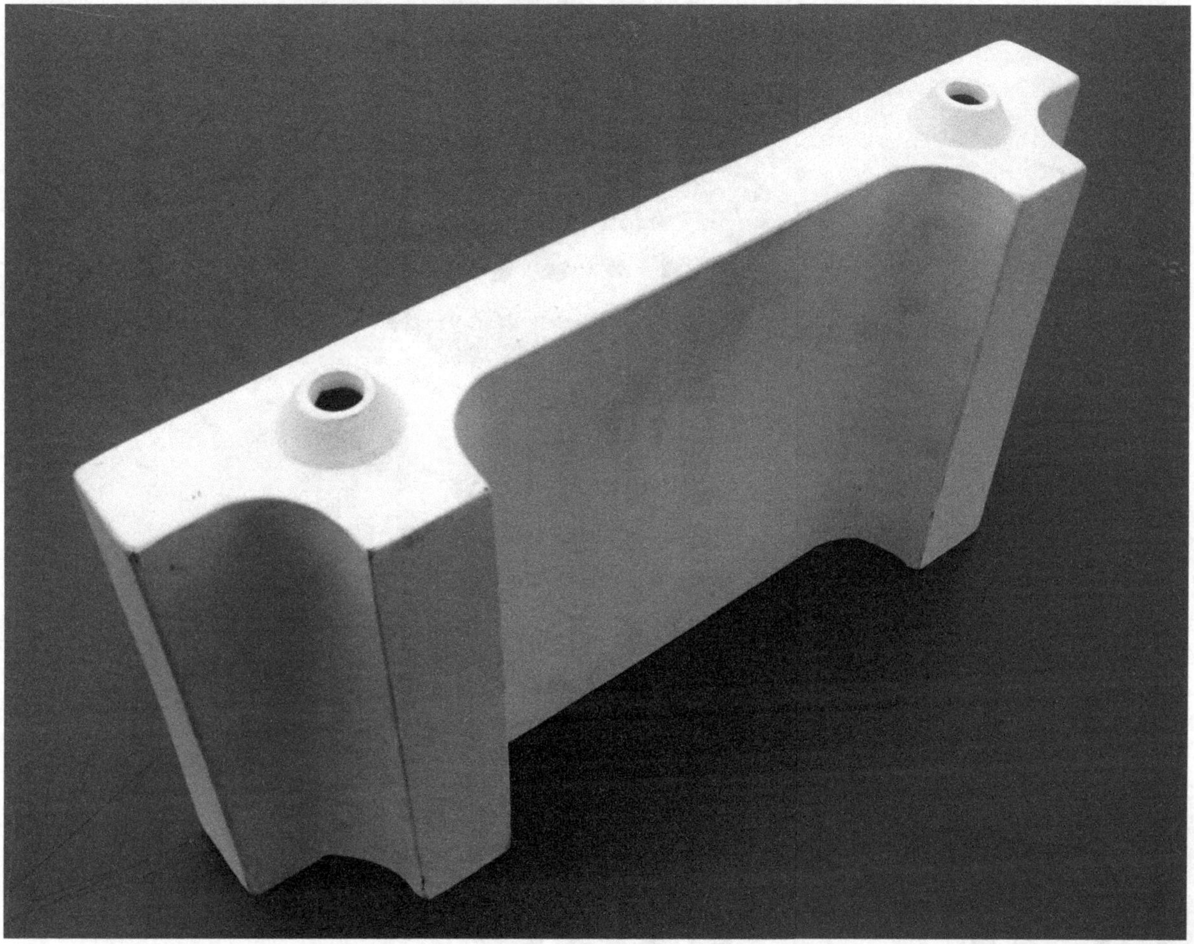

↑ **Fig 4.03.1** A porous ceramic evaporator developed as part of the EvapCool research project. These hollow ceramic bricks are slip-cast and designed to be filled with water. The components were manufactured by Elsa Ceramiche, Florence, Italy.

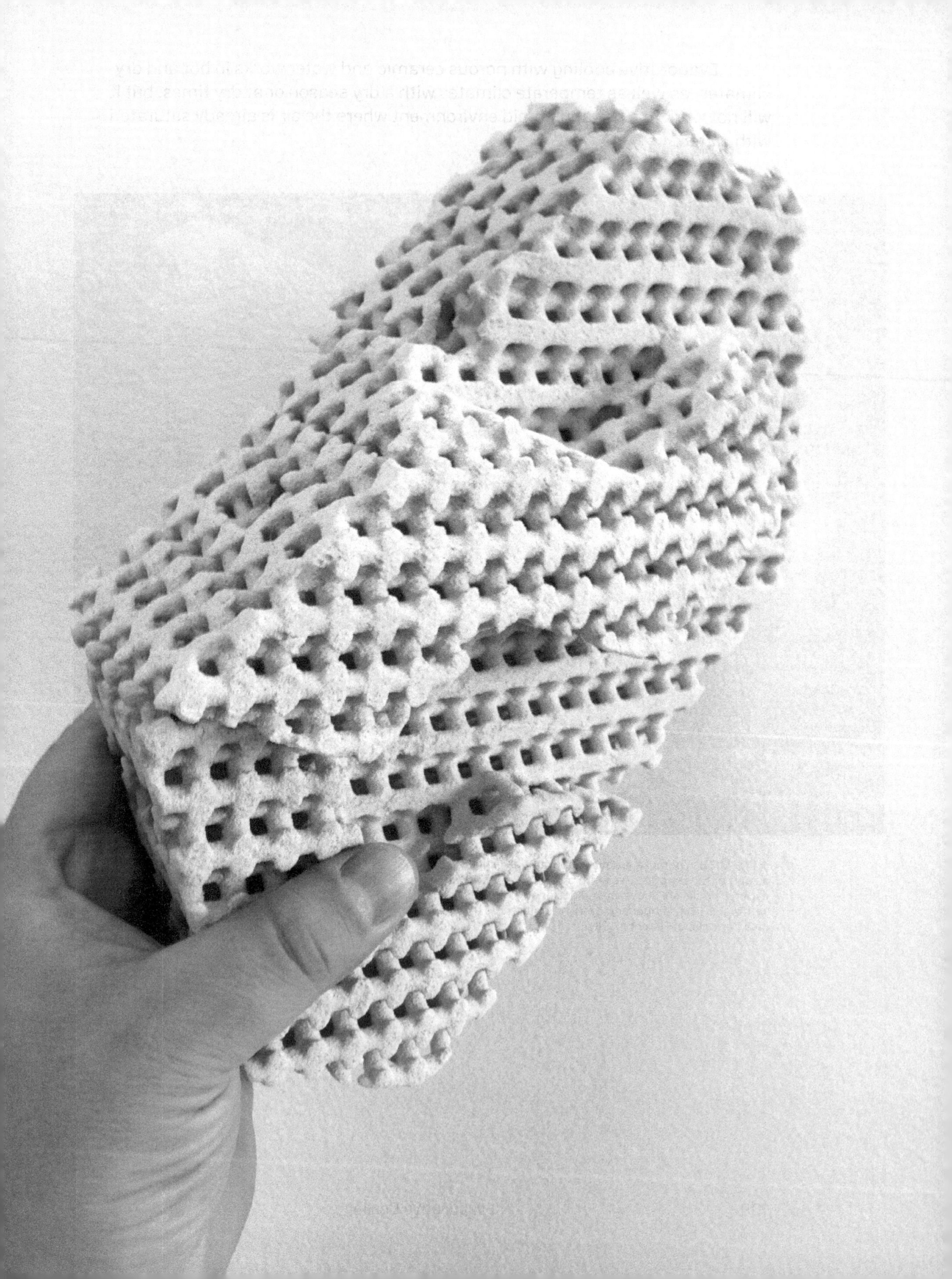

↑ Fig 4.03.3 The 'Cool Brick' 3D printed porous ceramic brick by Emerging Objects.

← Fig 4.03.2 The hollow ceramic bricks are designed as a modular system that can interconnect.

4.04	**Heat Pump (Air Source) – Bunhill 2 Energy Centre**
	Location: London, UK
	Designers: Ramboll, Cullinan Studio, McGurk Architects, Colloide

'The Greater London Authority estimate there is enough heat wasted in London to meet 38% of the city's heating demand. With the expansion of district heating networks this could rise to 63% of demand by 2050.'[62]

– Ramboll

This ground-breaking scheme, the first of its kind in Europe, is designed to utilise waste heat generated by London Underground trains running on the Northern Line, and provide heating for local homes, offices and leisure centres, while simultaneously helping to cool the underground network. Commissioned by Islington Borough Council, Bunhill 2 is an expansion of its pioneering district heating scheme (Bunhill Heat and Power Network, launched in 2012), and will provide affordable (and low-carbon) heat for 1,350 homes, a school, a swimming pool and other community buildings.

As part of the existing underground train network there are a series of ventilation shafts situated across London. One of these is located on the remains of the disused City Road Station, which is the site for the new energy centre. The centre houses a 500 kW ammonia heat pump driven by the heat recovery from a heat-exchanger coil within the ventilation shaft, recovering lost heat generated by Northern Line underground trains. The warm air of between 18 and 28°C created by trains, people and other ancillary machinery travels up the ventilation shaft and is drawn through a heat pump by a fan. The heat pump captures heat from the warm exhausted air, via a closed-loop water circuit in the ventilation shaft. This hot water is used to heat a gas, which is then put through a compressor, generating more heat for the water supply. The consultant engineers Ramboll undertook a feasibility study that confirmed this source of waste heat could be exploited by heat pumps, which would capture the waste heat in the ventilation shaft and upgrade it to approximately 80°C and then distribute it through insulated pipes to nearby buildings. In addition, the 2 m diameter fan installed in the ventilation shaft can also be reversed in the summer months to help with cooling the underground tunnels.

Transport for London, which operates London Underground and is one of the scheme's partners, has subsequently undertaken a survey of 56 more ventilation shafts in London to assess the potential of each for the capture of waste heat. To celebrate this innovative project, Cullinan Studios and McGurk Architects have designed a perforated metal cladding through which some of the heat-recovery machinery is visible, and which incorporates a cast-aluminium relief by Scottish artist Toby Paterson linking the centre and the community it serves.

→ **Fig 4.04.1** The Bunhill 2 Energy Centre, City Road, Islington. The thin-sheet steel cladding is perforated to allow interested passers-by to view the technology, as well as allowing good air exchange for the heat-exchange process to work. Islington Council.

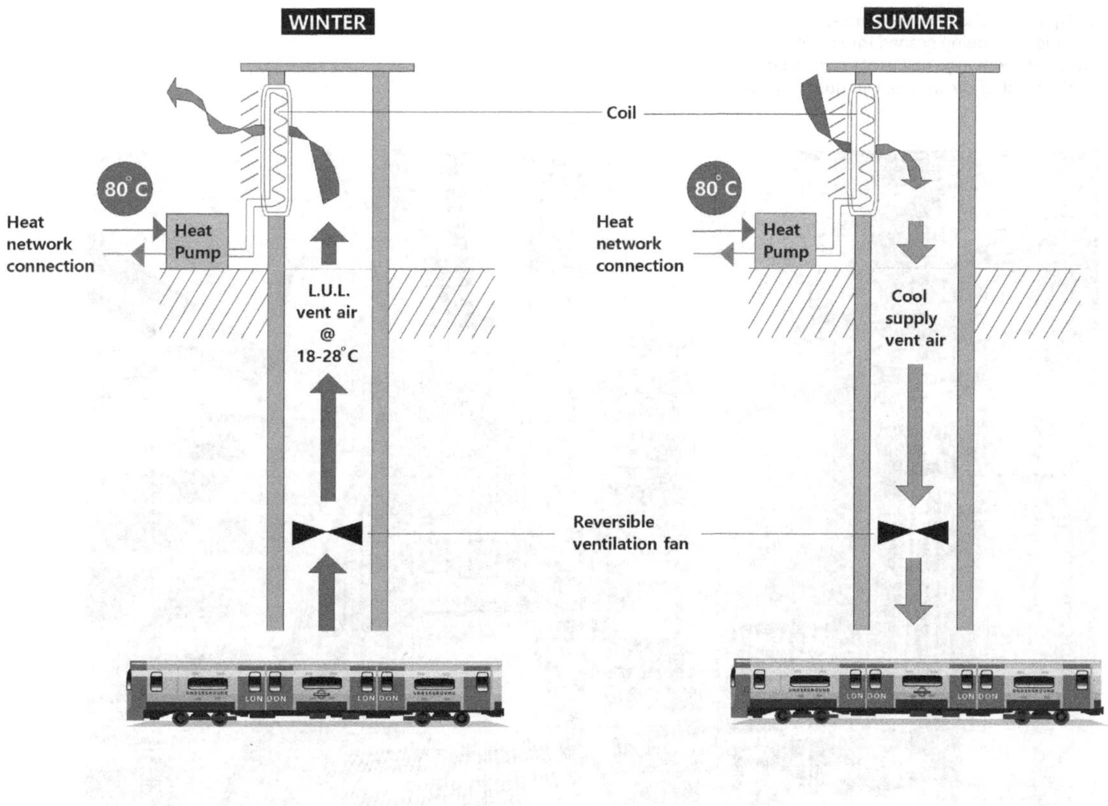

↑ **Fig 4.04.2** Diagram explaining how the Bunhill 2 (waste) heat recovery process operates in summer and winter.

↑ **Fig 4.04.3** The insulated hot water storage tank being craned into position. The heat-exchange coil vents can be seen on the right of the image. Islington Council.

↑ **Fig 4.04.4** Internal view of the heat exchange equipment. Islington Council.

↑ **Fig 4.04.5** View inside the underground train ventilation shaft showing the reversible fan, which can draw up hot air or push down cool air to power Bunhill 2 and help mitigate air temperatures on the underground railway system. London Underground.

4.05

Heat Pump (Ground Source): Energy Piles®

Designer: Skanska

'The temperature in the ground at around 15 m depth is equal to the mean annual air temperature.'[63]

– Rybach and Sanner

A ground source heat pump (GSHP) uses 'ground loops' of pipes buried 1–2 m underground. The pipes are filled with water and antifreeze, and when this liquid is pumped it can extract heat or coolth from the ground – for larger buildings, vertical boreholes can be used. The GSHP exchanges heat with the ground, and the deeper you go the more stable the temperature is. In the winter (when below ground is warmer than the above-ground air temperature) you can extract heat energy to heat a building, and in the summer that process can work in reverse, extracting coolth from the earth to provide building cooling. The length of ground loop or number of boreholes depends on the size of the building that needs to be heated or cooled. An interesting side-effect of the heat-exchange process, which uses the relative coolth of the ground to provide cooling to the building in summer, is that a GSHP will slowly warm the ground in time to provide heating in winter when the process is reversed.

Construction firm Skansa has pioneered the use of thermal piling, or Energy Piles® and Energy Walls®, which integrate the pipework of a GSHP into the concrete pile foundations and retaining walls of a new building. Large infrastructure projects such as Crossrail have used these new Energy Piles® to reduce heating and cooling demand for new underground stations in London. Energy Piles® and Energy Walls® contain a pipe loop filled with a water–glycol mixture and connected to a heat pump. In winter, the pumped water mixture extracts heat energy from the ground, which is converted to a higher temperature via the heat pump to provide heating within the building. A temperature differential from the Energy Piles® of between 5 and 6°C can meet the heating and cooling requirements of a building.

Other kinds of heat pumps include air source heat pumps (ASHPs), which absorb heat from the outside air to heat homes and hot water, and water-sourced heat pumps, where the running water of a river has been used to heat and cool large buildings. ASHPs use refrigerant liquid which has a much lower boiling point when compressed, and they can still extract heat when air temperatures are as low as -15°C. Bunhill 2 (see page 112) utilises an ASHP.

→ **Fig 4.05.1** Steel reinforcement cage for concrete pile foundations being prepared with closed loops of tubing attached.

SKANSKA

4.06	**Heliostats: Rjukan Sun Mirrors**
	Designer: Martin Anderson with Bosch Rexroth

'It's a kind of health project to promote the wellbeing of the people living in the dark.'[64]

– Martin Anderson

Rjukan is a small, remote town in Norway, 170 km west of Oslo. It was established between 1905 and 1916 by the engineer and industrialist Sam Eyde, who constructed a huge dam and hydroelectric generator to power the production of potassium nitrate fertiliser (saltpetre) through a novel method called the Birkeland–Eyde process. Rjukan is situated in a valley, and the northern latitude means that in winter the sun is very low, so between 28 September and 12 March it does not shine on the 3,400 inhabitants of Rjukan.

In 1913, Eyde had proposed to build a mirror to reflect sunlight into the town from the top of a nearby mountain, but his idea never came to fruition. Instead he built a cable car that took people to the top of the mountain for their regular dose of vitamin D. However, one hundred years later saw the realisation of the Rjukan Sun Mirrors. This remarkable project, led by artist Martin Anderson, and engineered and constructed by Bosch Rexroth, uses the sun-tracking technology of a heliostat, more commonly seen in desert solar energy projects. There are three polished steel mirrors, each with an area of 17 m² and weighing 500 kg. The movement of the mirrors is powered by photovoltaic (PV) panels as well as a small wind turbine, and their altitude and azimuth position is adjusted every few seconds to keep sunlight focused on Rjukan. The mirrors are fixed 450 m above the town, and they illuminate 600 m² of the town square, including the statue of Sam Eyde. The temperature is increased locally by between 3 and 5°C by the reflected sunlight, and locals congregate to feel the sun on their faces, along with tourists intrigued by this engineering spectacle. The Rjukan Sun Mirrors follow in the footsteps of the small mountain town of Viganella in the Antrona Valley, Italy, where in 2006 then-major Pierfranco Midali made it his personal project to bring light to the central square, and he installed a large 5 x 8 m sun-tracking mirror in the hills above the town.

↑ **Fig 4.06.1** The three heliostats being installed 450 m above the town. The Bosch Rexroth control system computes the position of the sun and uses linear drives to align the mirrors so that the reflected rays of the sun illuminate the town square.

→→ **Fig 4.06.2** View from Rjukan town square with sunlight reflected from the mountain.

VERDENSARV
NOMINERT

4.07	**Passive Solar Heating: Zome House**
	Location: Albuquerque, New Mexico
	Designers: Steve Baer and Holly Baer – Zomeworks

'It's not very exotic or earthshaking to fill 55-gallon drums with water, paint them black and place them in the walls of a home for use as solar collectors ... but it works.' [65]

– Steve Baer

This elegantly simple passive solar heating system utilises the thermal capacity of water to store heat energy from sunlight. The climate of New Mexico, characterised by hot days and cool nights, can be moderated in buildings by capturing, trapping and releasing heat energy as required. Steve Baer is an American inventor who has pioneered the use of passive solar technology. In the mid-1960s he moved to Drop City in Colorado, which had become home to a countercultural 'hippy' community. Baer, who had been inspired by Buckminster Fuller, wrote and published *Dome Cookbook* in 1968, a 'do-it-yourself' instruction manual for self-build geodesic dome housing. Baer went on to develop his own polyhedral structural system called a 'Zome', a name combining 'zonohedron' and 'dome.' His experience of building geodesic domes was that it was a complex task to make a simple shape, whereas the Zome was a complex-looking shape that was easier to build.

In 1972, Baer moved to Albuquerque, New Mexico, where he built the iconic Zome House, which comprises 11 separate but interconnected Zome units. The Zomes are fabricated from large sandwich panels consisting of two aluminium skins laminated to a cardboard honeycomb core and insulating foam. Internally, adobe wall partitions are employed for thermal mass. The south facade is what Baer describes as a variation on the trombe wall, and consists of four single-glazed end walls. The largest are 3 x 3 m, behind which sit a 5 x 5 or 4 x 5 grid of 245 litre (55 gallon) steel barrels 95% full of water. The 90 barrels in total contain 20,000 litres. The barrels are painted black, sit on a steel rack and absorb the free solar energy throughout the day and re-radiate the stored heat into the house at night. In addition, this simple but novel system employs a series of additional insulating shutters, which can be winched closed to trap the heat at night. The inside of the shutter (when open) reflects sunlight on to the water-wall, maximising solar gain. During the summer, when the temperature in the rooms is hotter than the water in the barrels, the water just absorbs the difference, keeping the rooms cool and providing a natural form of air-conditioning.

↑ Fig 4.07.1 Steve and Holly Baer's Zome House, showing the south-facing water-wall, Albuquerque, New Mexico, 1972.

↓ Fig 4.07.2 The north wall of the Zome House, made from foam-filled insulated aluminium panels. Albuquerque, New Mexico, 1972.

4.08	**Thermal Labyrinth: Federation Square**
	Designer: Atelier Ten

'Thermal storage is starting to get talked about more, as a complement to electricity storage ... batteries to go with our PV (photovoltaic) systems are one way to store energy, but thermal batteries are often (mostly) less expensive and store a different kind of energy.'[66]

– Paul Stoller

Federation Square, Melbourne, Australia, was designed by Lab Architecture Studio with Atelier Ten. The centrepiece of the building is a large winter garden 'atrium' space that uses an innovative double skin of glass and steel to provide solar shading and prevent solar gain, as well as directing excess heat through the layered facade and up and out of the building. However, arguably the most remarkable technical innovation at Federation Square is invisible, sandwiched between the subterranean rail tracks and the plaza. The designers have created a 'thermal labyrinth' that is used to moderate the internal building temperature and act as a (thermal) battery pack, storing the coolth of the night air during summer so that it can cool incoming air during the day. The labyrinth is created by a grid of concrete walls which air is drawn past. The air movement is primarily driven by the stack effect of hot air being more buoyant, rising up and out of the atrium and drawing in air below, through the labyrinth.

↑ **Fig 4.08.1** Thermal labyrinth at Federation Square in Australia. The crenellated concrete increases the surface area and thus improves heat-exchange between air and the thermal mass of the concrete.

The concrete walls of the labyrinth provide good thermal mass, and they have been crenellated to increase their surface area and improve heat exchange from (battery) wall to air. The basic idea is that air is exposed to a large surface area of concrete on its way into the building by passing at low velocity down a tunnel. The principle also works in reverse, with cool night air being heated by the concrete, which has warmed throughout the day. The big diurnal temperature change from night to day allows this passive system to run on a tenth of the energy of a conventional air-conditioning system, and during local heatwaves in 2014 when external temperatures measured at over 40°C for four consecutive days the atrium was kept at a hot (but not uncomfortable) 28°C without the use of refrigeration.

→ **Fig 4.08.2** Thermal labyrinth at Federation Square in Australia under construction. The short concrete walls are only fixed to one of the side walls, forcing the air to snake around the thermal mass of the concrete.

↓ **Fig 4.08.3** Diagrammatic plan view of the (below-ground) thermal labyrinth at Federation Square, Melbourne. If you follow from red to blue arrows you can see how the air is cooled before being brought up to the public spaces.

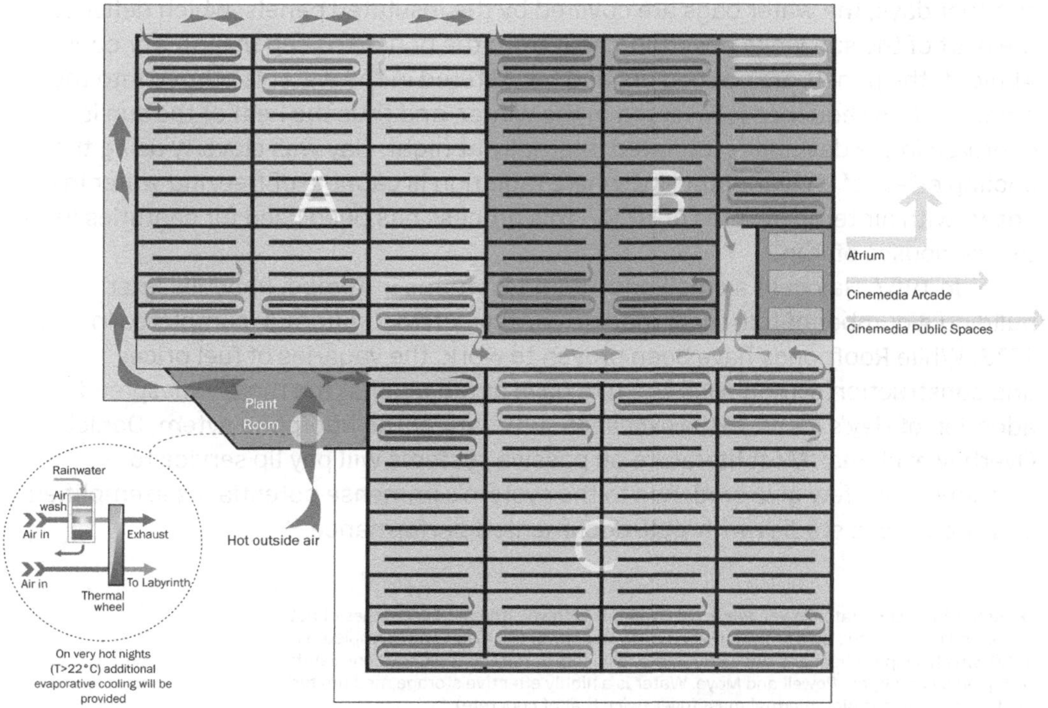

4.09

Thermal Storage: The Roofpond

Inventor: Harold Hay

'Water is the cheapest and most efficient heat storage material for buildings. Its fluid convection provides an outstanding advantage over the heat lag of solar materials.'[67]

– Harold Hay

While water is less than half the density of concrete, its specific heat capacity (its ability to store heat) is four times greater. The chemist and inventor Harold Hay pioneered a way to heat and cool a house with sunlight and water. Hay was adamant that simplicity was the key to his invention of the Roofpond and Skytherm systems, which used rooftop water tanks (or water bags) to moderate the internal temperature of a house. If you study Hay's various registered patents it is clear that one of his great innovations is the use of movable thermally insulated panels (movable thermal barriers). The other was to capitalise on the excellent thermal storage capacity of water. While water is less than half the density of concrete, its specific heat capacity (ability to store heat) is four times greater.

The Roofpond system incorporates a large mass of water in troughs or water bags into the flat roof of a house. The roof is covered by a movable layer of thermal insulation panels, which when deployed expose the water to the sky. During hot summer days, the water bags are covered by the insulated panels, which deflects the heat of the sun while absorbing heat from the house to keep the interior cool. At night, the panels are opened up, and heat stored in the water is purged into the night air. This sequence is reversed in the winter, and thus the heat of the sun is captured in the day and re-radiated internally at night. Hay was cleverly using the cooling effect of a clear night sky, where radiation is capable of freezing water in a desert with air temperatures of 10°C – this process has been used for centuries in the ice houses of Iran.

In 1967, Hay built a small one-room test home in Tempe, Phoenix, later building a number of full-scale models in Atascadero, California, completed in 1973. While Roofponds have been proven to work, the vagaries of fuel prices and construction orthodoxies seem to have acted against the more widespread adoption of Hay's ideas. In his excellent summary of the Roofpond sytem, Daniel Overbey explains: 'Most literature on passive systems will pay lip service to roofponds, but few give credence to the system's immense potential as exemplified by various case studies with well-documented performance.'[68]

→ **Fig 4.09.1** Accumulator Tower, Pimlico, London. This tower stores 2,500 tonnes of hot water and is part of the UK's first Combined Heat and Power (CHP) network completed in 1950, which supplies heat and hot water to the residents of the Churchill Gardens Estate designed by architects Powell and Moya. Water is a highly effective storage medium for heat energy and has high thermal mass (over twice that of concrete).

WATNEYS

4.10 Wind Catcher: Yazd, Iran

'There are no passive structures in the world as effective as these towers at cooling the internal climate of buildings.'[69]

– Dr Susan Roaf

Wind catchers can be found in different forms across the Middle East – in Egypt, India and Pakistan. The wind catchers *(badgir)* of Yazd in Iran were constructed in the summer quarters of houses and designed to mitigate extremely high air temperatures of 40°C and provide internal ventilation. The oldest existing towers date back to the 14th century, but there is good evidence to suggest they were used as far back as 400 BCE.[70]

The wind-catcher towers in Yazd take many cross-sectional forms, and though most are rectangular in plan, there also are hexagonal and octagonal towers. The performative design of the tower types also varies, with some single-aspect shafts facing the prevailing winds of north or northwest, but the most common types of badgir are internally subdivided with diagonal partitions. This internal subdivision of the towers into separate shafts allows prevailing (and cooler, higher-altitude) winds to be driven down into the building on the windward side while simultaneously ventilating the internal space with air drawn out of the tower on the leeward side – depending on the wind direction, this process is reversed. Most of the wind towers are no more than 3 m higher than the roofline of a house, but exceptional examples such as the octagonal tower at the villa at Bagh-e-Dowlatabad in Yazd are over 30 m high. The towers are constructed from dried mud or fired bricks, and are finished in an earth and straw render.

The climate in Yazd is hot and dry, and some examples of the towers are connected to basement areas in the houses, which provides access to the unique Yazdi underground canal system qanat and allows cool, moist air to be drawn up through the building. The towers are part of a constructed system built for human comfort in extreme heat that uses the natural flow of the wind, material properties and the large diurnal temperature change. The Historic City of Yazd was one of eight new sites to be inscribed on UNESCO's World Heritage List, 9 July 2017, and the citation explained that 'Wind-catchers, courtyards, and thick earthen walls create a pleasant microclimate'.

↑ **Fig 4.10.1** View of roofs with wind towers or badgirs in Yazd, 1976.

‘So that is another rule for the whole nature of architecture: it must create new appetites, new hungers - not solve problems, architecture is too slow to solve problems.’[71]

Cedric Price

Chapter 5: **Buildings**

The belief that architecture is too slow to solve problems, as put forward in the opening quote, seems like a useful provocation for the young designer. If we are very lucky, then might architecture at least provide new possibilities?

The conflicting criteria of a design project should always be thoroughly explored, and it is true that some of the most interesting architecture of the past was often closely aligned with a strong technological paradigm in the use of a new material of material process for its realisation. The issue of embodied energy is as important as that of energy in use, and architects, engineers and designers are rightly looking at the sourcing and provenance of materials as well as material efficiency and the circular economy, of which construction is a key part.

Weighed down by the bad decision-making and environmental and social disasters of their forebears, young designers should not be limited in their ambitions or discouraged by circumstance – it is difficult to believe that the wholesale improvement of our environment will be achieved by parsimony alone. The rediscovery of traditional and sometimes ancient vernacular technologies for the construction, heating and cooling of buildings is as exciting as the new bio-fabrication methods of literally growing buildings or their components. Digital tools for design, analysis and fabrication provide the basis for a total rethink of the way that we build, informed by nature and local materials, crafts and techniques. Regulatory controls and standards applied to construction are a useful means to ensure and improve safety or technical performance of a given building, but they are only one part of the picture: they do not guarantee the more complex qualitative enjoyment of architecture and construction.

The featured buildings are necessarily eclectic, and in each example we have tried to identify an embodied technology or environmental imperative that drives the design. In the case of BACA's Amphibious House, designing for change and adaptation was key, where the potentially catastrophic weather events of a flood can be mitigated with a building that moves – not geographically, but up and down, lifted by the water of a flood event. The Cork House is both an award-winning piece of architecture and an ongoing research project. With its singular construction made almost entirely from cork (the harvested bark of Portugese cork trees), it is a wonderful exploration of the technical and aesthetic properties of a remarkable and renewable farmed material. Buckminster Fuller's Dymaxion House and Enric Ruiz-Geli's ICT Building in Barcelona are technically more eclectic case studies, and their potency lies as much in their rhetorical power as the actuality of their construction. For each, there is a long list of novel material specifications, material efficiencies and new approaches to a dynamic building envelope. In Mick Pearce's Eastgate Centre, Hugh Broughton's Halley VI, Jean and Henri Prouvé's Maison Tropicale and the Mongolian Ger, we see buildings designed for specific and extreme climatic conditions. While Broughton's Antarctic research centre is in large part about shelter and protection from the weather, a series of hydraulic legs enable this building to move and relocate, prolonging its role, and it might be described as being between building and vessel. Similarly, the Mongolian Ger is specifically designed to be moved, and provides a home for nomadic herders in Mongolia. The useful deployablity of the ger is remarkable, as are its lightness and thermal properties. The Eastgate Centre's biomimetic inspiration presents a complex picture of environmental tuning and mitigation, where the thermal sophistication of a termite mound is studied, modelled and recast as a large office and shopping complex in Harawe. HANNAH's Ashen Cabin presents a small but potent prototype that uses new digital fabrication technology to make use of a construction material that would previously have been classified as waste material.

In Gianni Botsford's House in a Garden, he creates a largely buried house in a north-facing garden that is – counterintuitively – full of light. He continues to develop a sophisticated series of one-off projects born out of his graduate research work, which share a vicarious love of the (less than dependable) sunlight of northern Europe. And finally architect Scott Batty's own St Albans Family Home presents a valuable study the potential of the retrofitted home, which eschews wholesale demolition and replacement (with attendant waste and energy use) with a fine-grained refurb, which both improves the technical performance and spatial disposition of a house and serves as a living research project from which we can continue to learn.

This collection of buildings attempts to illustrate a range of projects that, through material composition, site specificity or technological ambition, present different models of ambitious environmental design. No single project is an answer to all environmental challenges, but these 'case studies' are usefully explicit and diagrammatic to serve as inspiration or provocation for future designs. In the case of Buckminster Fuller's Dymaxion House, this one-off prototype has often been derided as a failure because its planned roll-out as a housing 'product' failed to materialise. However, the ambition and questions that Fuller asked about the future of a house – its performance, material composition, engineering efficiency and construction, remain.

These building projects are necessarily emblematic, and the Cork House or the Amphibious House might be characterised as niche 'one-offs', but both of these buildings are the result of extensive and detailed technical research. In the case of the Amphibious House, one of its designers, Robert Barker (now of Stolon Studio) has been widely published for his work in designing for flood risk, contributing a new 'flood aware' chapter to the *Metric Handbook* as well as being a part of the BRE team for the Flood Resilient Repair Home at the BRE Innovation Park in Watford. The Cork House extends an idea of constructing a dwelling (more or less) out of a single building material, which is both weathering and thermal insulation and is not clad, covered or disguised inside or out. This project also employed complex robotic routing and machining to create the intricate kit of interlocking and watertight blocks. Cork has history as a construction material, but the 'all cork' signature of this building and its unique fabrication demand that we think again about the use, performance and application of this sustainably farmed construction material from Portugal. These building examples are just that: not part of a 'canon' of approved designs with a certain pedigree, but notable buildings that illustrate a range of approaches (both technical and programmatic) to sustainable environmental design.

5.01	**Amphibious House**	
	Designers: BACA – Robert Barker and Richard Coutts	
	Location: Marlow, Buckinghamshire	Completed: 2014

'Floods are among the most costly natural disasters in Europe. Their impact has grown steadily in the past decades due to the increase of population and built-up areas. Climate change is likely to affect the hydrological regimes in various world regions, with potential implications on the frequency and intensity of floods, and other weather-related hazards.'[72]

– Alfieri, et al.

The idea of the Amphibious House was to create a house that can float if it needs to. Rather than defend against flooding, this unusual house type employs a non-defensive approach that generates a new form of architecture in response to flood risk. The UK's first amphibious house was built on an island on the River Thames in Marlow, Buckinghamshire. The site was originally home to a small one-storey bungalow, and the clients wanted to create a three-bedroom family house. In order to comply with local planning requirements, the overall height of the building was limited, as was the plot size, and the designers decided to include a basement. In normal circumstances, because of the adjacency to the river, this would not have been technically feasible. The house was eventually designed over three floors, and it can cope with flood risk and will not increase flood effects on neighbouring sites. The site had no vehicular access, so the construction process was challenging.

The designers employed Archimedes' buoyancy principle, and calculated the displacement of their construction to know at what water level the house would begin to float. The house is designed for two positions – resting, and floating during a flood event. A concrete retaining wall creates a wet-dock for the house, which sits within the trough like a giant flat-bottomed boat. Guide rails are notched in the side walls of the house, with guide posts (known as dolphins) fixed to the foundations. The wet-dock is so called because the retaining walls are perforated and allow the ground and river water to fill the box and lift the building in tandem with rising river water in a flood situation. The Amphibious House is designed to cope with a 1.8 m flood level, and up to 2.5 m. Interestingly, one of the most complex technical challenges of the project was the flexible utility connection, which provides power, water and sanitation in an umbilical connection that needs to allow for movement while remaining operational. The designers of the house are also the co-authors of *Aquatecture: Buildings Designed to Live and Work with Water.*[73]

↑ **Fig 5.01.1** The UK's first amphibious house is built on an island on the River Thames in Marlow, Buckinghamshire. BACA Architects.

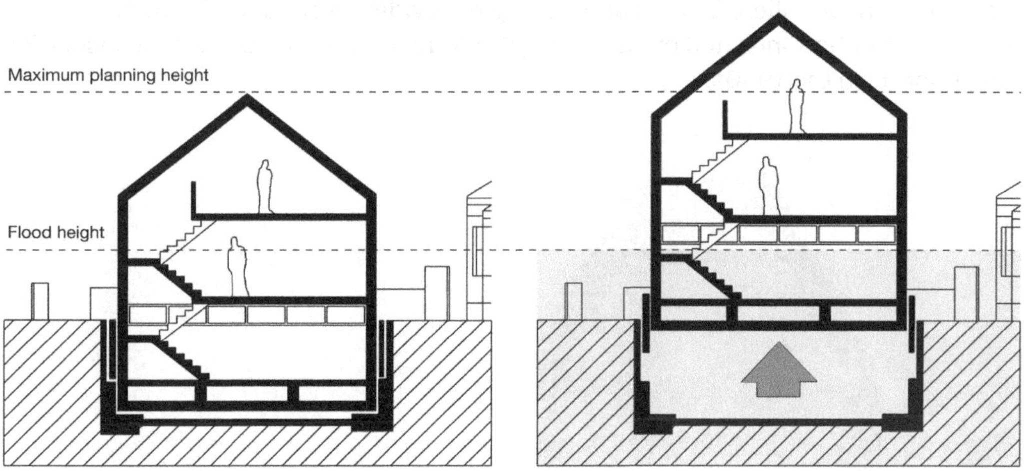

↑ **Fig 5.01.2** Diagram, showing how the Amphibious House floats and vertically lifts in the event of a flood. BACA Architects.

5.02	The Cork House	
	Designers: Matthew Barnett Howland, Oliver Wilton and Dido Milne	
	Location: Eton, Berkshire.	Completed: 2019

'... expanded cork is a remarkable, carbon-negative engineered plant-based material, made from cork waste.'[74]

– Oliver Wilton

In 2014 architect Matthew Barnett Howland and architect/researcher Oliver Wilton began researching and prototyping a novel construction technique that used blocks of expanded cork, assembled using a '... reimagining of historic dry-stone construction'.[75] Their work was prototyped at three scales: Cork Casket, Cork Cabin and ultimately the Cork House. This research project was driven by a shared desire to explore the future possibilities of plant-based construction and usefully employ the natural insulative (thermal and acoustic) properties of waste cork.

Cork is the harvested outer bark of the cork oak tree, which grows in the western Mediterranean basin, notably Portugal. The cork bark is stripped from the trees every decade and used in its pure form (after drying) for wine bottle stoppers. Waste cork is typically granulated, and with the addition of binders is used as lower-priced bottle stops as well as for insulation panels and a host of other industrial products. Barnett Howland and Wilton chose to use a pure expanded cork agglomerate, which does not use any binders and is formed from granulised cork waste with superheated steam. This process was powered by biomass waste, so the cork blocks are classified as carbon negative, in that they sequester more carbon than is used in their production over a lifetime. Cork has been used in construction for millennia, with archaeological evidence of its use in the Nuragic civilisation of Sardinia, and most recently (at industrial scale) for thermal insulation and flooring in the 1930s.

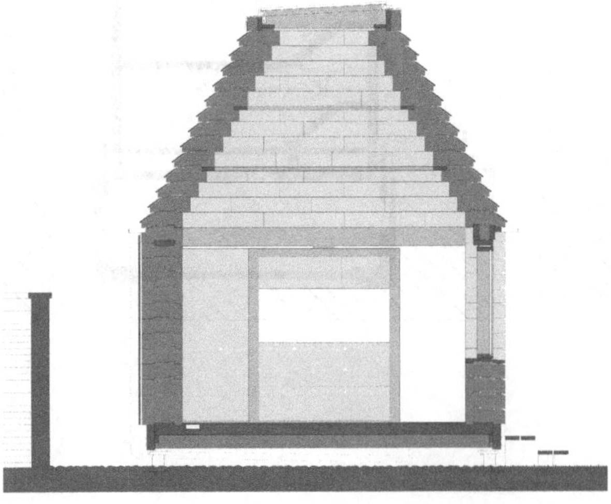

← **Fig 5.02.1** Cross-section drawing of the Cork House, which shows how the solid cork walls and roof blocks are CNC machined and interlocking. Matthew Barnett Howland, Oliver Wilton and Dido Milne.

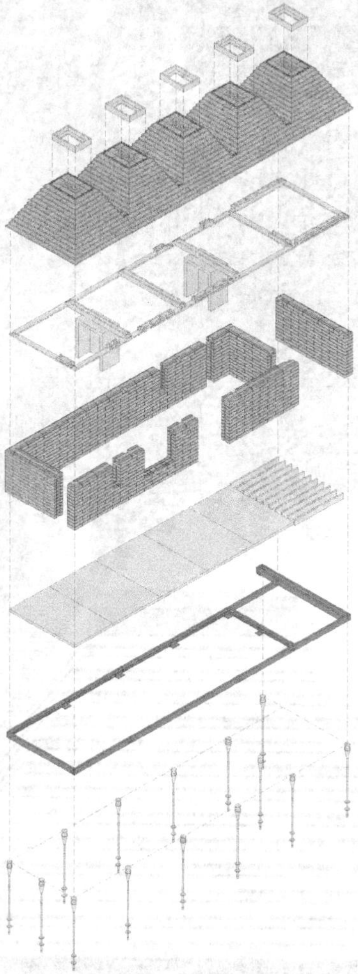

← **Fig 5.02.2** Exploded isometric drawing of the Cork House, showing steel screw-pile foundations, timber floor structure and then the layered cork walls and five corbelled cork pyramidal roof profiles with glass skylight 'lids'. Matthew Barnett Howland, Oliver Wilton and Dido Milne.

→→ **Fig 5.02.3** Completed Cork House, with designer Matthew Barnett Howland sitting on the front step. Note the copper guttering and flashing detail between the pyramidal roof profiles.

What is unique about the Cork House is that its entire construction was conceived as a cork substrate, so that the structure of the walls and roof, thermal insulation, water and airtightness (the building envelope) are all achieved through the careful assembly of expanded cork blocks. The precision jointing of these blocks with the use of CNC routing and machining of the individual components enabled the designers to successfully create this remarkable building. The walls and roof of the Cork House comprise 1,268 interlocking (dry-jointed) cork blocks, which sit on an engineered timber deck supported by steel screw-piles that provide a concrete-free foundation. Door and window frames are engineered timber, and the roof includes strips of cedar weatherboarding after extensive testing proved this was required to repel driving rain. The iconic outer form of the house is generated by the corbelled form of this undressed compression structure. Internally a water sprinkler system was used for fire protection, as the designers were reluctant to line or internally clad the monolithic cork blocks. In like-for-like 'whole life carbon assessment' by Sturgis Carbon Profiling (SCP), the Cork House proved to have the lowest carbon emissions of any building tested by SCP, and was carbon negative at completion.

5.03	Dymaxion House	
	Designer: Richard Buckminster Fuller	Completed: 1948
	Location: Dearborn, Michigan (original location Wichita, Kansas)	Restored: 2001

'Efficiency = doing more with less. EFFICIENCY EPHEMERALIZES.'[76]

– Richard Buckminster Fuller

Dymaxion House was designed by the US architect, engineer, inventor and environmental designer Richard Buckminster Fuller as an alternative to the American Institute of Architects (AIA) optimum family home designs, which he calculated weighed 150 tonnes and were heated with fossil fuel. Fuller's original design for his Dymaxion House (1927) weighed in at an impressive 3 tonnes ($\frac{1}{50}$ of the weight) and was suspended off a central mast. Fuller believed that poor housing was 'responsible for practically all our ills', and a description of his original Dymaxion House given at an address to the Architecture League NY in 1929 described an earthquake- and flood-proof dwelling, utilising vacuum-insulated panels to providing a super-insulated environment. The house would employ the latest (non-petrochemically derived) bio-plastics made from casein (milk by-products), with the whole house being hypoallergenic and 'air-conditioned' through the central mast, with humidity controlled and dust filtered. Fuller's first Dymaxion House was designed and modelled but remained unbuilt. In 1940 Fuller designed an emergency shelter for the British government called the Dymaxion Deployment Unit (DDU).[77] The DDU was fabricated by the Butler Manufacturing Company and utilised a modified version of a circular-plan grain store, which Butler produced. The DDUs, although originally intended for the UK, were eventually launched in 1941 in the US, including the exhibition of a prototype at MoMA in New York, with approximately 100 finding their way to military installations across the rest of the country.[78]

In 1944, the second iteration of the Dymaxion House (also known as the Wichita House), was prefabricated by the Beech Aircraft Company in Kansas. The Wichita House was an 11 m diameter circular-plan 120 m² housing vehicle, made from prefabricated aluminium panels, supported on an earthquake- and flood-proof central mast. The house featured Fuller's patented Dymaxion Bathroom, a two-piece copper die-stamped pressing with water saving 'fog nozzle' technology which obviates the need for soap. The house also included the innovative 'ovolving' storage system and a rotating roof cowl for filtered air intake and extraction. The house weighed 3 tonnes, as per Buckminster Fuller's original designs in 1927. The Dymaxion (Wichita) House has now been restored, and is housed at the Henry Ford Museum in Dearborn, Michigan.

↑ Fig 5.03.1 The original prototype of the Dymaxion House was assembled in Kansas in 1948 and has become known as the Wichita House. In 1990 the Henry Ford Museum in Dearborn, Michigan, purchased the house and after a $1 million restoration project the house was put on permanent display in 2001.

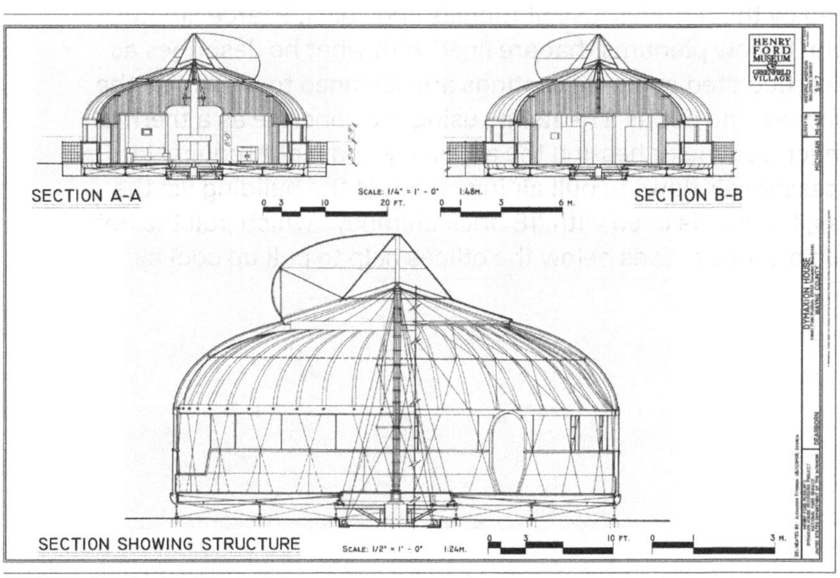

← Fig 5.03.2 Historic American Buildings Survey drawing of the Dymaxion House to mark its arrival at the Henry Ford museum.

5.04	Eastgate Centre	
	Designer: Mick Pearce	
	Location: Harare, Zimbabwe	Completed: 1996

'Whether the building has begun to attain a life of its own since occupation is a matter of judgement. This was an attempt to design a building based on a metaphor of a living system more like a termitary. An ecosystem not a machine for living in.'[79]

– Mick Pearce

The Eastgate Centre is a shopping and office complex located in central Harare, Zimbabwe, which opened in 1996. Architect Mick Pearce's ambition was to create a building that was as comfortable as a building with air-conditioning, but without using air-conditioning. Pearce studied the microclimate of the site location and used the natural environment to enable the building to cool itself. He employed the emerging discipline of biomimcry and biomimetics, which author and biologist Janine Benyus describes as '... a new science that studies nature's best ideas and then imitates these designs and processes to solve human problems'.[80] Pearce studied the large termite mounds of Zimbabwe to understand how the termites could so skillfully regulate the internal temperature of their home. Pearce then set about designing an analogue of this sophisticated natural system.

Because of the significant diurnal temperature change between day and night in Harare, Pearce decided to use night cooling and purge the building of the heat from the previous day, and then store the night coolth to cool the offices in the daytime. A cross-section of Eastgate shows two blocks alongside a central, covered atrium. Inspired by the termites' use of tunnels and voids, Pearce creates office floors formed with hollow plenums that are lined with what he describes as 'concrete teeth'. These articulated concrete castings are designed to maximise the surface area of the concrete and act as a heatsink, using the concrete as a thermal store and heat-exchanger, cooling or heating the air as day and night require. In order to create the necessary air flows to pull air in and out of the building via the heat-exchange process, the roof is lined with 48 brick chimneys which pull the hot air from the offices, and a series of fans below the offices help to pull up cool air from the lower atrium.

The highly articulated outer surface of the building is inspired in part by desert cacti, which use their large and crenellated surfaces to both self-shade and lose heat at night. The outer facades are also covered in plants, with natural transpiration creating local cooling. Following completion, environmental monitoring has demonstrated that Eastgate consumes less than 50% of the energy used in conventionally air-conditioned buildings, while achieving satisfactory comfort conditions for all but two of the 52 weeks of the year. Efforts were also made to employ local materials and skilled labour in the construction, and only 12% of the construction materials were imported.

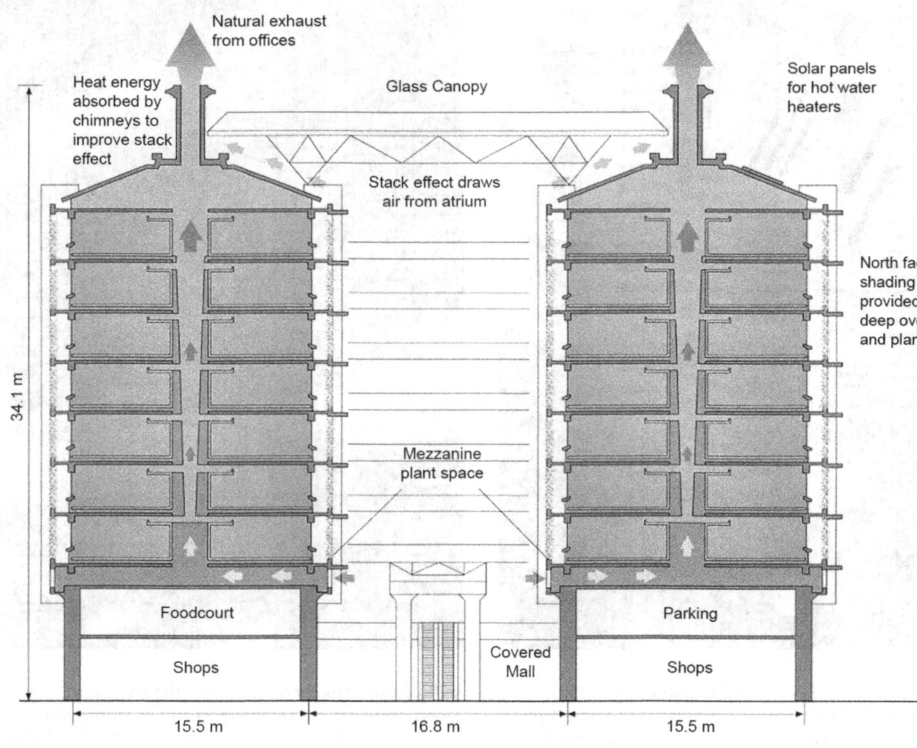

↑ **Fig 5.04.1** North–south cross-section diagram showing how the stack effect is integrated into the two blocks and helps pull air though floor plenums. The height of the chimneys creates the stack effect, as well as the heat absorbed in the surface of the chimney. The top profile of the chimney employs Bernoulli's law to increase wind pressure around the surface to help purge heat for the building. Mick Pearce Architects.

↑ **Fig 5.04.2** The east end of the building references the kopjies (granite stone outcrops) of Zimbabwe, and employs the crenellated (or prickly) surface morphology of the cactus to create a surface that resists absorbing heat in the day (because of self-shading) while efficiently releasing heat in the night-time because of maximised surface area. Mick Pearce Architects.

↑ **Fig 5.04.3** The long facades of the Eastgate Centre incorporate deep solar shading and planting, which protects the offices from direct solar gain and helps with local cooling via the transpiration of the leaves. Mick Pearce Architects.

→ **Fig 5.04.4** Internal view of the Eastgate Centre showing the giant roof truss and suspended lifts that do not touch the ground. The deep and narrow section restricts direct sun, keeping the internal atrium and shopping centre cool. The glass roof is held above the two office blocks to allow excess heat to escape. Mick Pearce Architects.

↓ **Fig 5.04.5** Precast concrete units that are used to form the office floors. Dentil (teeth-like) forms are cast on to the underside to improve heat-exchange and help remove heat from the offices by pulling air through a plenum under the office floors. Mick Pearce Architects.

5.05	Halley VI	
	Designer: Hugh Broughton Architects	
	Location: Various, Brunt floating ice shelf	Completed: 2013

'At Halley typical winter temperatures are below -20°C with extreme lows of around -55°C. There is 24-hour darkness for 105 days per year.'[81]

– British Antarctic Survey

Halley VI is the world's first re-locatable research facility. Completed in 2013, it was subsequently moved 23 km in 2017, to a new home on the Brunt floating ice shelf almost 1,500 km away from the South Pole. Working with infrastructure company AECOM, Hugh Broughton Architects won the competition to design the new Halley VI research station in Antarctica for the British Antarctic Survey. The research building consists of eight conjoined modules, raised up above the ground on hydraulic legs, each fitted with a ski. The legs are designed to be individually raised or lowered to overcome snow movement and accumulation, and the skis allow the modules to be moved if required.

Halley VI is orientated in a straight line, perpendicular to the prevailing wind. Snowdrifts form in the lee of the building, leaving the wind-blown side clear for access and vehicular movements. The centrally located red module contains the communal social and recreational areas, while the blue modules provide laboratories, offices, staff accommodation and plant rooms for generators and storage. The bridge link provides access to and through the modules, as well as containing power lines, water and drainage.

The individual modules consist of a steel space-frame chassis (on legs) with steel portal frames forming the superstructure, which is clad in large semi-monocoque glass reinforced-fibre polymer (GRP) composite panels with expanded foam insulation. The largest panels measure more than 10 x 3 m. The overall U-value of the building is 0.113 W/m^{2}K, very similar to that of a Passive House[82] construction. The GRP panels were fabricated in South Africa, where they were tested before being shipped to Antarctica on a special reinforced cargo ship. The modules were assembled in 12 weeks at Halley V, which could house the construction team. Once complete, the modules were towed 15 km inland to the (original) Halley VI site.

As a result of the success of the Halley VI project, which is able to withstand extreme weather conditions and physical relocation, Broughton has worked on a number of other research stations, including the Juan Carlos 1 Spanish Antarctic Base on Livingstone Island, completed in 2018. He is currently working on the redevelopment of Scott Base for Antarctica New Zealand on Ross Island.

↑ **Fig 5.05.1** Halley VI British Antarctic research station. The central red module provides social space including a canteen and library. Hugh Broughton Architects.

↑ **Fig 5.05.2** Night view of Halley VI, showing ice on the surface of the modules. Hugh Broughton Architects.

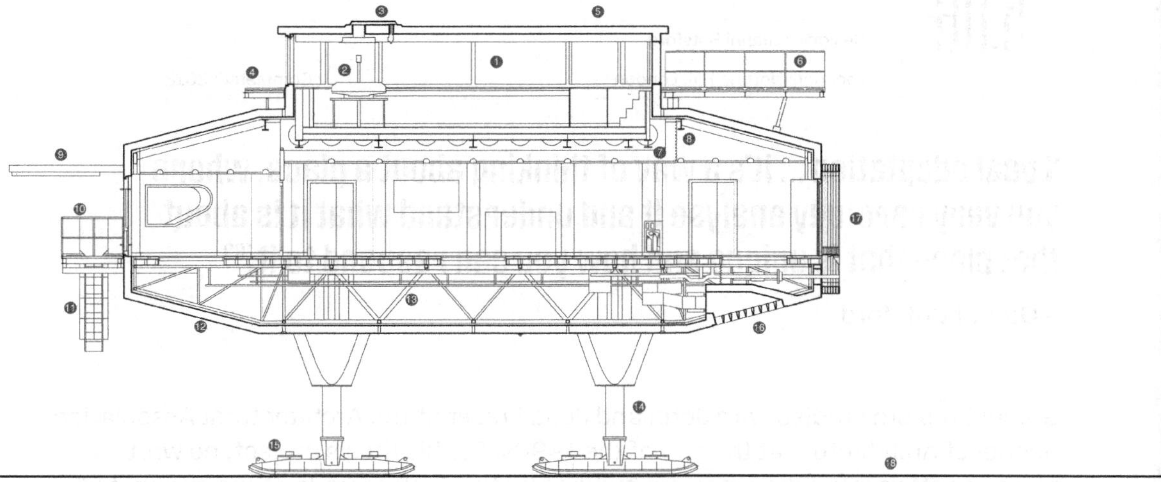

↑ **Fig 5.05.3** Cross-section of the science module showing the adjustable hydraulic legs and 'ski' feet. Hugh Broughton Architects.

5.06	House in a Garden	
	Designer: Gianni Botsford	
	Location: Notting Hill, London	Completed: 2018

'Local adaptation ... it's a way of thinking about a place, where you very carefully analyse it and understand what it is about that place that is unique and how you can respond to it.'[83]

– Gianni Botsford

Gianni Botsford studied with John and Julia Frazer at the Architectural Association School of Architecture at the end of the 1990s. For his thesis project, he wrote a piece of software (no drawings, no building) with which to understand sunlight at different times and locations. Forms were then generated by the software in direct response to specific environmental criteria. After graduating and establishing his own practice, Botsford's first project was The Light House, a commission for a large house in a hemmed-in, windowless and overlooked courtyard site. Botsford wanted to begin the project without any preconceived ideas and begin by analysing the site. The analysis lasted six months and, working with engineers Arup, he developed a unique three-dimensional mapping of sunlight levels and potential sun hours across the total buildable volume of the site. The simulations were mapped across 6,000 data points in an isospatial grid, and with this fine-grained data Botsford went on to organise spatial arrangements in relation to the sunlight requirements of the functions of the house, such as sleeping, working, gardening and so on.

Botsford has returned to exhaustive solar analysis of site in his most recent and award-winning private residence, House in a Garden. Botsford used a detailed three-dimensional and time-based solar modelling of the north-facing garden site in West London to generate ideas (or forms) that might respond to that information. The house is built in the shadow of its surrounding buildings, and had to reach out to where there was potential for sun. The complex compound curved roof form of the resultant pavilion sits atop two glazed walls pulling light in from the sides and rises to an oculus, optimally positioned to trick light down into the building. The roof is an exquisite piece of prefabricated glue-laminated (glulam) timber frame skinned with copper, and the positioning of the apex of the oculus is the result of Botsford's creative solar surveying. The house is mostly subteranean and the uncanny qualities of interior light two storeys underground are testament to Botsford's acuity as both exemplary designer and researcher. The design of the pavilion roof is the answer to the questions of sunlight and privacy in an overshadowed and overlooked site. In a lecture at the University of Westminster,[84] Botsford explained that his ideas of 'local adaptation' are a form of contextualism, which do not aesthetically borrow from the stylings of neighbouring buildings but learn from the environmental conditions of a given site.

↑ Fig 5.06.1 The external profile of House in a Garden reaches out to where there is light in the back garden of a London townhouse. The roof is clad in a thin layer of copper with standing seam joints. Gianni Botsford Architects.

↑ **Fig 5.06.2** Internal view showing the underside of the glulam timber roof structure. Gianni Botsford Architects.

↑ **Fig 5.06.3** Assembly of the glulam roof structure, which was originally prefabricated and assembled in Italy, before being disassembled into sections, shipped and re-assembled on site. Although the structure was 3D modelled, the carpenters used full-scale printouts and traditional craft techniques (more akin to boatbuilding) to create the complex double-curved (and twisted) glulam timber struts. Gianni Botsford Architects.

5.07	**Ashen Cabin**	
	Designers: HANNAH	
	Location: Ithaca, New York	Completed: 2019

'The universe as we explore it has got feedback for the architect - for what materials we use, in terms of saving the planet.'[85]

– Eva Jiricna

The HANNAH design studio, which is led by co-principals Sasa Zivkovic and Leslie Lok, worked with students from Cornell University to design and construct this experimental off-grid residence in upstate New York. Uniquely, the project uses wood infested by the emerald ash borer beetle, which leaves the wood distorted, tightly curved and unsuitable for traditional saw milling.

This beetle-infested wood would normally be destroyed or left to rot, but HANNAH devised a unique cutting process, which utilises 3D scanning technology in combination with a robot-mounted bandsaw that is capable of cutting precise slices of the curved timber members. The use of these new 3D scanning technologies in conjunction with cutting and milling tools and processes could help to extend our understanding of usable construction materials and the optimisation of their use. The designers have deliberately embraced the non-standard timber components in the design of the cabin, which is lined inside and out with the lapped planks or log sheathing. The curved ends are used to dramatic effect in accentuating the protruding timber plywood windows. With the use of this new robotic-based fabrication technology, the designers explain that they have turned a waste wood product 'into an abundantly available, affordable, and sustainable building material'.[86]

The structural timber carcass of the cabin is built around a 3D-printed concrete platform and chimney. The 3D 'printing' is an additive fabrication process, using a robot arm that can precisely lay down (or pipe) a continuous cementitious layer. This process can create large lightweight concrete forms, which do not require any formwork (and attendant waste) and minimise the use of cement. A similar 3D additive fabrication process can be replicated with clay. The precision of this fabrication process is used in conjunction with the structural design to optimise and minimise material use, while providing maximum strength. Hollow 3D-printed blocks can be subsequently filled with concrete (or other aggregate) if structural (or thermal) mass are required. Fabricators are currently exploring different methods of structurally reinforcing 3D-printed concrete, experimenting with metal 'staples' and fibrous reinforcement threads. Nascent design-research projects like the Ashen House provide design inspiration as well a glimpse into a possible construction future, where the increasingly ubiquitous technology of real-time scanning and robotics are combined to re-imagine the processes of design, fabrication and construction.

↑ **Fig 5.07.1** Ashen Cabin, Ithaca, New York, 2019.

↑ Fig 5.07.2 Ashen Cabin, Ithaca, New York, 2019.

→ Fig 5.07.3 Detail of the Ashen Cabin showing how the curved planks of ash are used to form the structure and cladding.

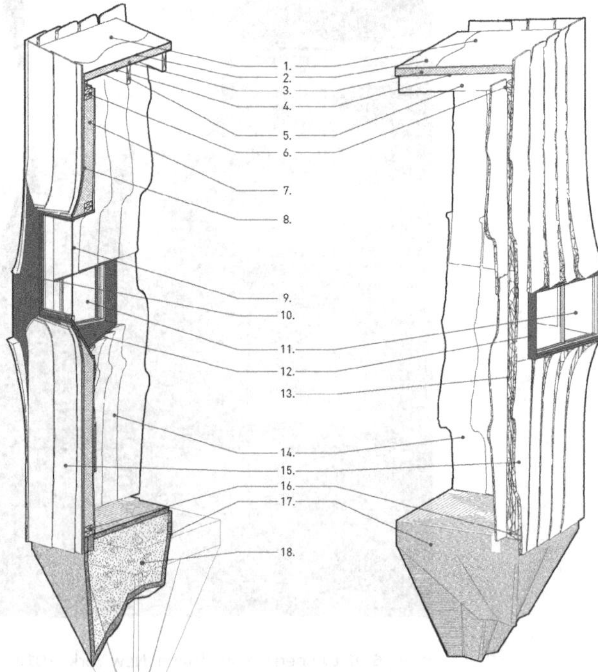

1. EPDM ROOF MEMBRANE
2. ROOF COVERBOARD
3. RIGID INSULATION
4. PLYWOOD SHEATHING
5. 2X6 WOOD RAFTER
6. 2X4 INTEGRAL WOOD TOP PLATE
7. CLOSED CELL SPRAY FOAM INSULATION
8. INTEGRAL CORRUGATED DRAINAGE PLANE
9. FIXED GLAZING
10. PLYWOOD SPANDREL
11. OPERABLE GLAZING
12. PLYWOOD WINDOW BOX
13. INTEGRAL LOG POST
14. INTERIOR LOG SHEATHING
15. EXTERIOR LOG SHEATHING
16. 2X4 INTEGRAL WOOD BOTTOM PLATE
17. 3D PRINTED CONCRETE FORMWORK
18. POURED CONCRETE INFILL

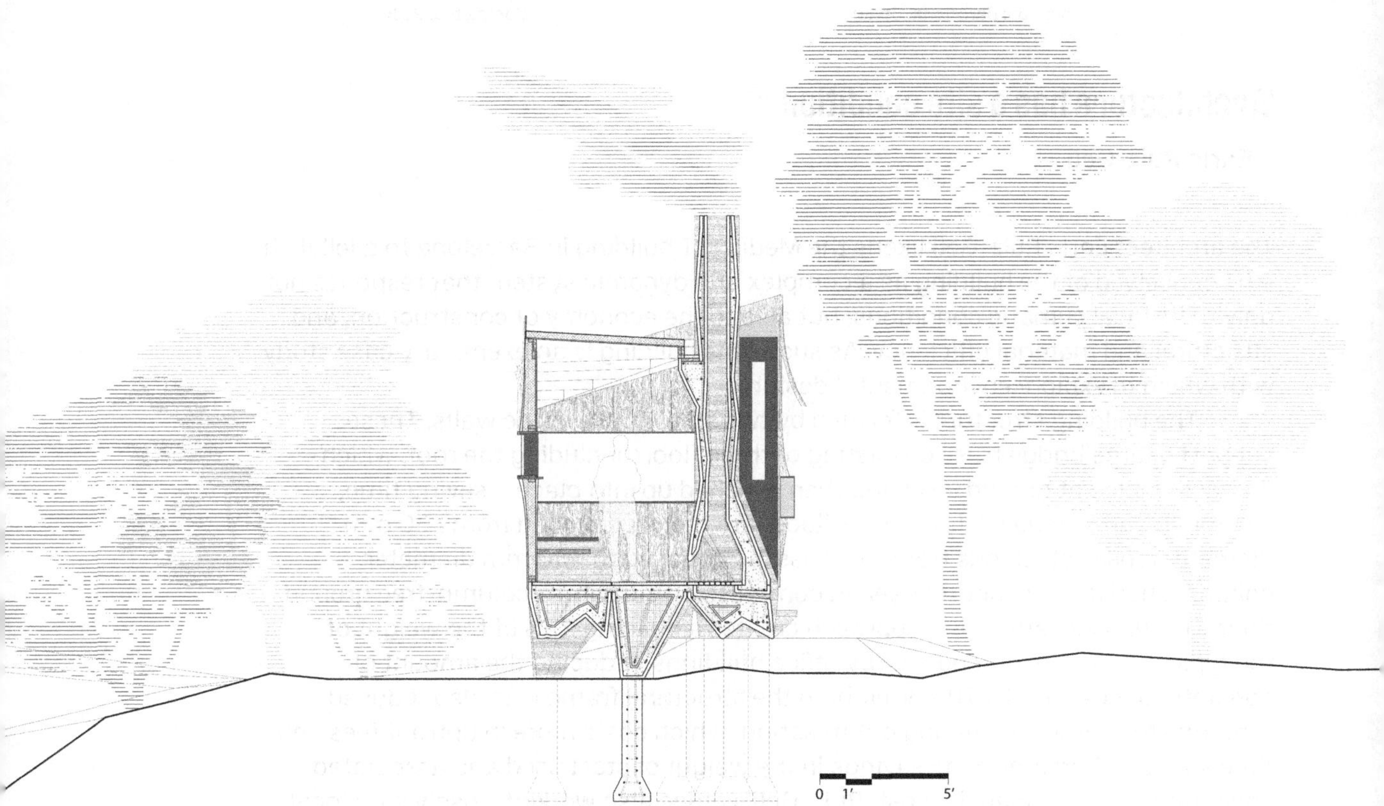

↑ Fig 5.07.4 Cross-sectional diagram showing the layering and build-up of the cabin floor, walls and roof.

5.08	Media ICT	
	Designer: Enric Ruiz-Geli – Cloud 9	
	Location: Barcelona, Spain	Completed: 2010

'Architecture has a site condition.'[87]

– Enric Ruiz-Geli

The architect Enric Ruiz-Geli likens the Media ICT building in Barcelona to a jellyfish – he conceived of the building as a complex and dynamic system that responds not only to its local climatic conditions, but also to the economy of construction, and structural and material efficiency. As such, this building is an exemplary case study with which to explore environmental design.

The building structure is formed by two steel-framed side walls. These support a large bridge truss consisting of three floors including the roof, which was assembled at ground level and then winched up into place – saving time, scaffolding and money. A further six floors are then suspended from 150 mm diameter tensile steel rods from the truss (as opposed to 500 mm diameter columns, had these supports been in compression), leaving a column-free ground floor. This unusual structural approach creates a building 25% of the weight of the typical concrete-framed nearby office buildings, reducing the amount of concrete foundations by 70%. Weight in the structural frame was also reduced through structural engineering optimisation, which costs more in upfront fees and time spent, but creates huge savings in the weight of steel used and associated environmental and financial cost. Ruiz-Geli's office also worked closely with local steel fabricators, directly sending them digital templates for plasma cutting the steel and thus using ubiquitous digital tools to re-establish design at the heart of the construction process.

Ruiz-Geli exclaims that 'Architecture has a site condition', and as such, each facade of Media ICT is required to perform differently. A south-facing facade in Barcelona can receive solar energy of 3200 W/m^2 every hour, whereas the north facade will receive 200 W/m^2 every hour. On the south facade, Ruiz-Geli created a double wall with glass and an array of ethylene tetrafluoroethylene (ETFE) cushions in front to control solar shading. Each of the ETFE cushions consists of three layers, shaped by low-pressure air and held in aluminium frames. The individual cushions are separately connected to an Arduino microprocessor and respond autonomously to the heat of the sun, with the skin opacity controlled through the differential movement of offset-printed layers of ETFE. The west facade uses nitrogen and an oil-based 'vaping' machine to control the opacity of vertical ETFE cushions, with the vaporised fog pumped into the building-height cushions, to create a huge translucent facade.

Other key technical features of the building include a network of hundreds of local sensors to control light, heat and humidity that work in conjunction with the facade, heat and lighting systems. The building roof features a garden to encourage biodiversity, alongside photovoltaic cells and a rainwater collection system, and all internal structural steelwork is painted with bioluminescent paint – which, like jellyfish, glows in the dark.

↑ **Fig 5.08.1** The South facade of Media ICT is covered with Arduino controlled ETFE cushions which can respond to heat and light levels and provide active shading.

→→ **Fig 5.08.2** Detail of Media ICT facade showing ETFE cushions with printed (light reflecting spots).

5.09	**Mongolian Ger (Yurt)**
	Researcher: Urangua Sodnomjamts
	Location: Sükhbaatar Province, Mongolia

'It is a round structure of easily dismantle-able walls, poles and a round ceiling covered with canvas and felt, tightened with ropes. The ger was designed to be light enough for Mongolian nomads to carry, flexible enough to fold up, pack and assemble.'[88]

– UNESCO

The ger (or yurt, as it is also commonly referred to) is an ingenious deployable dwelling that has existed for thousands of years. The Nomadic herders of Mongolia would move seasonally for protection against the weather and to find the best grazing. In 2017, National Geographic estimated that over half of the three million population of Mongolia lived in gers.[89]

The dimensions of gers vary, and are determined by the number of folding lattice panels that form the external wall. Each panel (khana) is made from between 70 and 80 (larch or birch) timber lathes approximately 2.4 m in length. The lathes are then either bolted or tied together with leather strips as a two-way lattice grid, which can be folded and deployed like a concertina for ease of assembly and transportation. The most common type of ger consists of five khanas and creates a building 5.8 m in diameter with a wall height of 1.7 m, rising to over 2.5 m at the crown. A ger of this size can be assembled in an hour by a family and dismantled in half an hour. The roof structure is formed by rafters that hook over the edge of the khana and slot into the crown or toono in the centre of the roof. The toono provides ventilation (in and out) for the ger, as well as daylight, and also acts as a smoke vent, although more recently this is via a steel chimney connected to a stove. The construction of a ger also utilises two central columns (bagana), which hold the toono in place during the placing of the rafters and can be removed after assembly depending on the size of ger.

The outer skin of the ger is made from two or three layers of sheep's wool felt and covered with waterproofed canvas. Three loops of rope around the walls secure the covering, and in hot weather the fabric and felt side covering can be lifted up at the bottom edge for increased ventilation. Tradition dictates that the single door will face south, and that when the ger is moved it leaves little trace or damage to the ground, with no need for foundations or ground anchors.

It is difficult to overstate the technical acuity of the ger: its form, lightness, strength and stability given the high winds of the Central Asian steppe, and its thermal performance using natural materials in a climate with a huge temperature range from 24°C to -28°C.

In 2013, the 'traditional craftsmanship of the Mongol Ger and its associated customs' was recognised as a part of the Intangible Cultural Heritage of Humanity by UNESCO.

↑ **Fig 5.09.1** A nomadic family of Sükhbaatar Province and their two gers, Mongolia, 2017.

↑↗→ Fig 5.09.2 Small-scale (1:20) model showing the construction sequence and the structural frame of a ger.

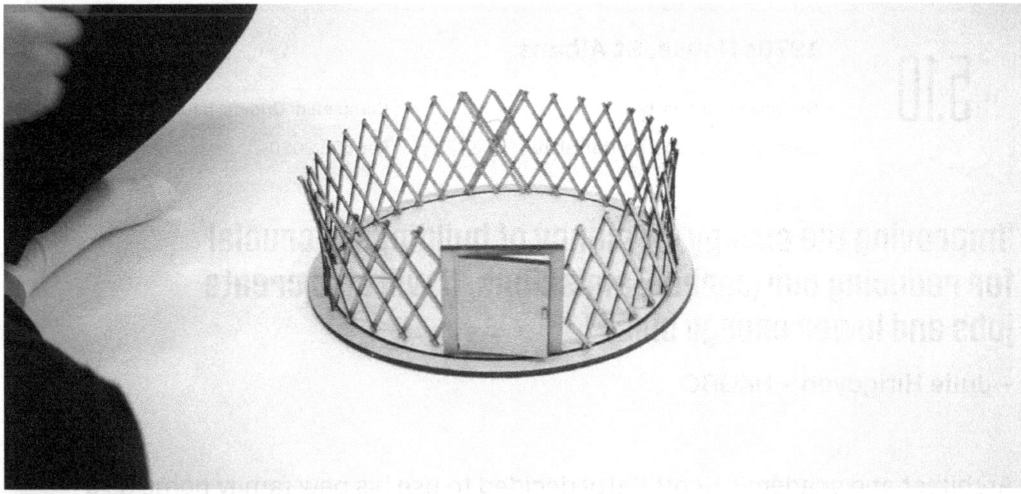

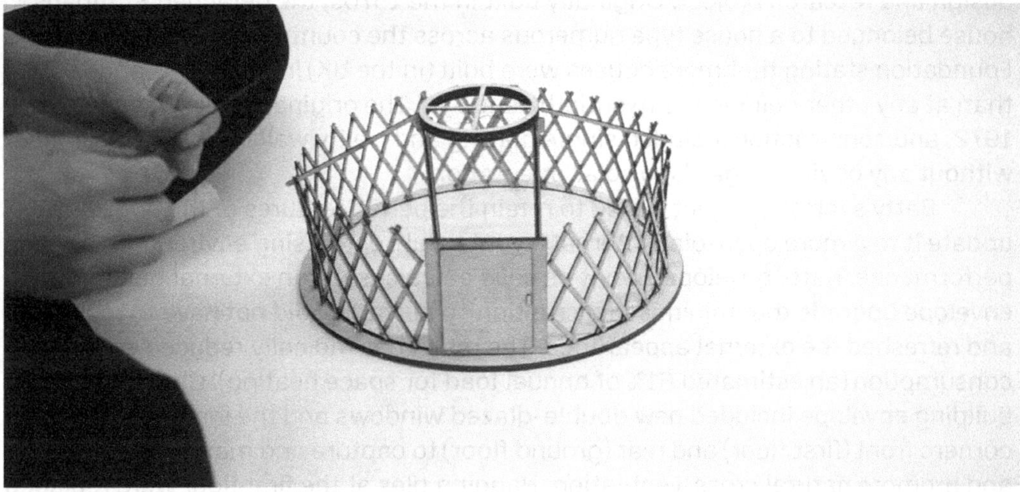

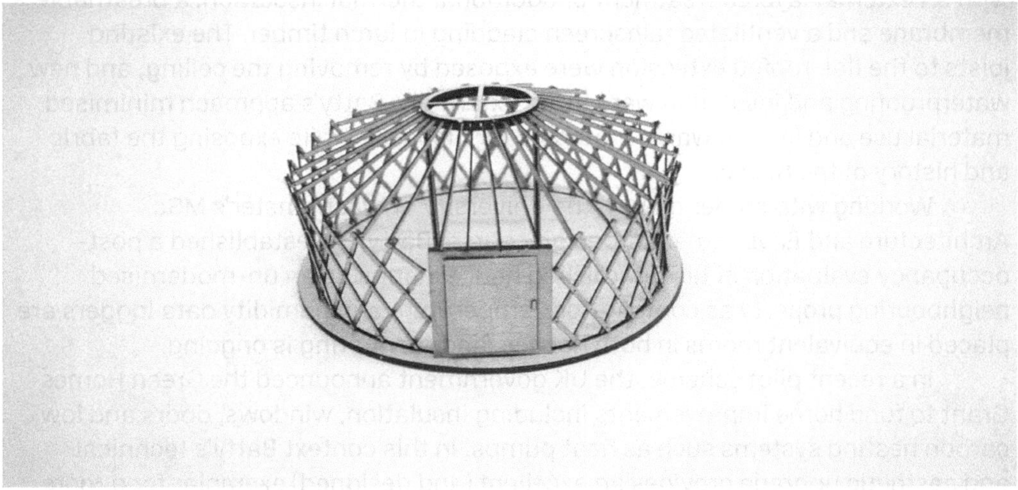

5.10	1970s House, St Albans	
	Designer: Scott Batty	Completed: Original house 1972
	Location: St Albans, Hertfordshire	Retrofit: 2020

'Improving the energy efficiency of buildings is crucial for reducing our (carbon) emissions. It will also create jobs and lower energy bills'[90]

– Julie Hirigoyen – UKGBC

Architect and academic Scott Batty decided to use his new family home as a design and research project. Originally built in the 1970s, the detached St Albans house belonged to a house type numerous across the country, with the NHBC Foundation stating that more houses were built (in the UK) in the 1960s and 1970s than at any other point in the twentieth century.[91] The original house was built in 1972, and construction included single glazing and cavity walls, and was designed without any obvious regards to solar orientation.

Batty's retrofit project aimed to retain the period features of the house, update it to a more open-plan internal layout, while optimising environmental performance. Batty developed what he calls a 'tea cosy' – an external building envelope upgrade that minimised disruption so his family did not have to move out, and refreshed the external appearance. The result has radically reduced energy consumption (an estimated 61% of annual load for space heating). Changes to the building envelope included new double-glazed windows and the insertion of glazed corners front (first floor) and rear (ground floor) to capture and maximise solar gain and promote natural cross-ventilation. Hanging tiles at the first floor were replaced with an external layered treatment of additional thermal insulation, a breathable membrane and a ventilated rainscreen cladding in larch timber. The existing joists to the flat-roofed extension were exposed by removing the ceiling, and new waterproofing and insulation were fitted externally. Batty's approach minimised material use and limited waste materials for disposal, while exposing the fabric and history of the house.

Working with students from the University of Westminster's MSc Architecture and Environmental Design course, Batty has established a post-occupancy evaluation of his refurbished house alongside an un-modernised neighbouring property as comparator. Temperature and humidity data loggers are placed in equivalent rooms in both houses, and monitoring is ongoing.

In a recent pilot scheme, the UK government announced the Green Homes Grant to fund home improvements including insulation, windows, doors and low-carbon heating systems such as heat pumps. In this context Batty's technical and aesthetic upgrade provides an excellent (and designed) exemplar for a more widespread retrofitting of an existing UK housing stock, which is poorly insulated and carbon-intensive to heat.

→ **Fig 5.10.1** Diagram showing the addition of the 'tea cosy' wrapping of the first floor and ground floor garage. The garage will be converted to living accommodation in a planned second phase.

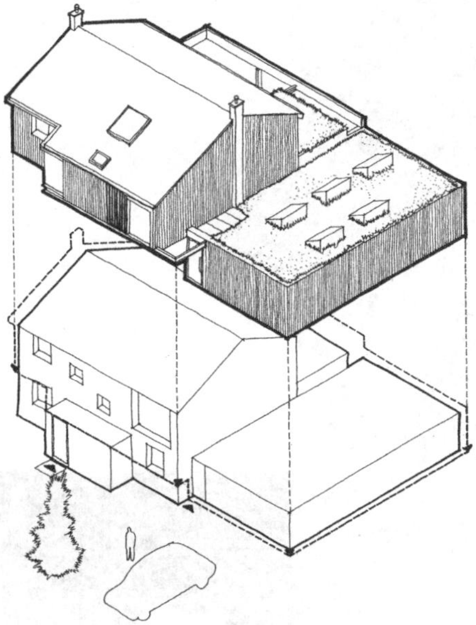

↓ **Fig 5.10.2** Front elevation of the house post retrofit, with an original un-renovated 1970s house in the background.

→→ **Fig 5.10.3** Rear elevation of the house post retrofit, with the architect pictured planning his next move.

Afterword

When you are teaching technology in a school of architecture it is useful to have exciting design projects that illustrate the principles by which something works. *Environmental Design Sourcebook* is an attempt to highlight a range of design approaches, issues and technologies with which to develop sustainable designs in our age of climate change. Within the field of architecture and construction the sustainability agenda has recently shifted to focus on the embodied energy of construction materials and processes, in addition to the 'in use' energy it takes to heat and cool buildings. This realignment presents an interesting challenge for the designer, as it demands a thoughtful approach to resources and their provenance, and associated local questions of climate, available labour and skills. The case studies included in this book are a mixture of contemporary, old and even ancient, and it seems important that our knowledge of available design and technological approaches should not be limited by what is in our immediate purview. The generalist pursuit of architecture is best when it looks beyond simple aesthetic or stylistic difference and extends to include all appropriate knowledge and understanding in the service of a client.

Learning from the locals is a recurring theme in the book, which relates to both climate and inhabitants. Local adaptation through design and invention is real knowledge, and the question of how we can better understand the history of vernacular building to develop contemporary sustainable architecture and design is central. The book begins with principles of climate and human comfort, and an encouragement to establish your own understanding of environmental factors and building physics. Solar geometry might be easily modelled and illustrated, but comprehending it is more difficult. Architect Gianni Botsford's interest in solar geometry began while he was a student, and his work continues to explore the dynamic relationship between the sun, earth and architecture. His knowledge is not finite or definitive, but an ongoing exploration of the qualities of sun and daylight through his architecture. While the designer should understand the regulatory numerics of acceptable light and temperature levels in buildings, they should also have a sense of what those numbers look and feel like in reality. If we reduce design to a set of generic measurements, we have not fully exploited its potential to create transformative environments that do not damage the planet and are more than the sum of their parts.

We should embrace all the available tools for the study of our environment. New digital real-time modelling apps and measurement tools enable us to quickly study and analyse key environmental factors such as sunlight, solar geometry, temperature, thermal performance, sound pollution and air quality. These powerful tools can provide useful and immediate feedback, confirming (or denying) design assumptions, and helping to create a better-informed and site-specific sustainable architecture. The sustainability of a design project or any given technology can be understood in a number of ways, and the broadening (or expanded field) of the sustainability agenda should reasonably include ecological, economic and social factors – benefiting building inhabitants, the natural habitat and the local economy, through jobs and training. We should also understand sustainability through 'wellness', and how the making of places, environments and products can affect personal health. Good design with respect to access to natural light, fresh air and noise mitigation is essential, as is the thoughtful specification of low-carbon and non-toxic construction materials. The design of heating, cooling and ventilation systems should form an integral part of our design approach, both qualitatively and quantitively. The Bunhill 2 scheme in Islington, London illustrates how, through technical innovation and local need, inexpensive, low-carbon heating can be provided by 'borrowing' the waste heat from an underground railway system. Environmental design should be inspiring, optimising the use and application of natural resources through good engineering, programmatic invention and technical innovation. The collective endeavour of sustainable design is illustrated by the rapidly expanding (and recently established) networks across the fields of engineering that provide a great source of knowledge exchange about low- and no-carbon approaches to design and construction in view of climate change. Case studies throughout this book also document the innovations of individual entrepreneurs who have led the way with a specific technology or design approach, and we should celebrate these pioneers who have challenged the orthodoxy of their disciplines and led with new ideas and approaches. The earth's resources are finite, but innovation and invention are not, and as designers we must continually remind ourselves what the nature of the design challenge is, and how history, technology or imagination can inform a thoughtful and sustainable design approach.

Further Reading

Bakker, C., *Trespassers: Eco-Efficient Design,* 010, Rotterdam, 1999.

Beukers, A., *Lightness: The Inevitable Renaissance of Minimum Energy Structures,* 010, Rotterdam, 1998.

Bini, D., *Building with Air,* Bibliotheque McLean, London, 2014.

Broome, J., *The Green Self-Build Handbook,* Green Books, Cambridge, 2007.

Brown, G.Z., Sun, Wind & Light: Architectural Design Strategies, John Wiley and Sons, New York, 2014 (third edition).

Burberry, P., *Mitchell's Building Construction: Environment and Services,* Longman, London, 1997.

Daniels, F., *Direct Use of the Sun's Energy,* Yale, New Haven, 1970.

Francis, E., Ford, B. and Schiano-Phan, R., *The Architecture and Engineering of Downdraught Cooling: A Design Source Book,* PHDC Press, 2010.

Fuller, R. Buckminster, *Nine Chains to the Moon: An Adventure Story of Thought,* Birkhäuser, Basel, 2019.

Fuller, R. Buckminster, *Critical Path,* St. Martin's Press, New York, 1981.

Givoni, B., *Man, Climate and Architecture,* Elsevier Science Ltd, Amsterdam, 1969.

Khan, L. and Easton, B., *Shelter,* Shelter Publications Inc., California, 1973.

Krausse, J. and Lichtenstein, C., *Your Private Sky, R. Buckminster Fuller: The Art of Design Science,* Lars Müller Publishers, Baden, 1999.

Krautheim, M., Pasel, R., Pfeiffer, S. and Schultz-Granberg, J., *City and Wind – Climate as an Architectural Instrument,* DOM Publishers, 2014.

LeCuyer, A., *ETFE Technology and Design,* Birkhauser, Basel, 2008.

McLean, W. and Silver, P., Air Structures, Laurence King, London, 2014.

McLean, W., *Quik Build: Adam Kalkin's ABC of Container Architecture,* Bibliotheque McLean, London, 2008.

Nicholls, R., *Low Energy Design,* Interface Publishing, Oxford, 2002.

Oswalt, P. and Kossak, F., *Well-Tempered Architecture: Concepts for Green Office Buildings,* Aedes, Berlin, 1992.

Otto, F., *Finding Form,* Edition Axel Menges, Stuttgart, 1995.

Rudofsky, B., *Architecture Without Architects,* Doubleday, New York, 1964.

Rudofsky, B., *The Prodigious Builders: Notes Toward a Natural History of Architecture with Special Regard to Those Species that are Traditionally Neglected or Downright Ignored,* Harcourt, New York, 1977.

Silver, P., McLean, W., *Introduction to Architectural Technology,* Laurence King, London, 2013 (second edition).

Tirone, L., *Construção Sustentável,* Orem dos Arquitectos, Lisbon, 2012 (second edition).

Todd, J., *Healing Earth,* North Atlantic Books, Berkeley, 2019.

Watts, A., *Modern Construction Envelopes,* Springer Verlag, Vienna, 2011.

Notes

1 Frei Otto, *Finding Form,* Edition Axel Menges, Stuttgart, 1995, p 17.
2 UN Environment and International Energy Agency, 'Towards a zero-emission, efficient, and resilient buildings and construction sector. Global Status Report', 2017.
3 'Why there is a shortage of sand', *The Economist,* <https://www.economist.com/the-economist-explains/2017/04/24/why-there-is-a-shortage-of-sand>, 2017 (accessed 28 March 2020).
4 Richard Buckminster Fuller, *Critical Path,* St. Martin's Press, New York, 1981, p 208.
5 Beth Bennett-Britton, *SCHOSA Conference: Beyond Building Performance,* RIBA, 9–10 April 2015.
6 William McLean, 'McLean's Nuggets', *Architectural Design,* 77(2), 2007, p 140.
7 A.K. Mishra, M.G.L.C. Loomans and J.L.M. Hensen, 'Thermal comfort of heterogeneous and dynamic indoor conditions – An overview', *Building and Environment,* 109, 15 November 2016, pp 82–100.
8 Andy Ford, *SCHOSA Conference: Beyond Building Performance,* RIBA, 9–10 April 2015.
9 Livia Tirone, *Sustainable Construction: Efficient Solutions for the Mediterranean Climate,* Tirone Nunes, p 18.
10 H.G. Wells, *A Short History of the World,* Macmillan, 1922, p 3.
11 Richard Buckminster Fuller, Larry King radio show, 1983.
12 L. Pérez-Lombard, J. Ortiz and C. Pout, 'A review on buildings' energy consumption information', *Energy Build,* 40(3), 2008, pp 394–398.
13 Megan Davies Wykes, 'The effect of an indoor-outdoor temperature difference on transient cross-ventilation', *Building and Environment,* 168, 15 January 2020.
14 John Cage, *Silence: Lectures and Writing by John Cage,* Wesleyan University Press, Connecticut, 1973, p 3.
15 The WELL Building Standard™ is administered by the International WELL Building Institute™, which focuses '... exclusively on the ways that buildings, and everything in them, can improve our comfort'.
16 Farrington Daniels, *Direct Use of the Sun's Energy,* Yale University Press, New Haven, 1974, p 243.
17 Harold Hay, 'Natural Comfort Systems', in *Proceedings of the ASC/AIA FORUM '75 SOLAR ARCHITECTURE,* 26–29 November, ed. G. Franta, Arizona State University, 1975, pp 4.1–4.9
18 Ibid.
19 'Steve Baer and Holly Baer: Dome Home Enthusiasts', *The Mother Earth News,* July/August 1973.
20 Julian F.V. Vincent, 'Biomimetics in architectural design', *Intelligent Buildings International,* 2014, p 9. DOI: 10.1080/17508975.2014.911716
21 György Kepes, *Language of Vision,* Dover, New York City, 1995, p 80.
22 Daniels, *Direct Use of the Sun's Energy,* p 242.
23 Natsai Audrey Chieza, 'Fashion has a pollution problem – can biology fix it?', TED@BCG, Milan, October 2017.
24 Allison Dring, 'All Things Connected', Kohler Design Forum, London, 7 January 2019.
25 Culture.PL, 'Artists', https://culture.pl/en/artist/zbigniew-oksiuta/ (accessed 1 August 2020).
26 Frei Otto, *Finding Form,* Edition Axel Menges, Stuttgart, 1995, p 48.
27 Johanna Lehne and Felix Preston, *Making Concrete Change: Innovation in Low-Carbon Cement and Concrete,* The Royal Institute of International Affairs, Chatham House, 2018, p v.
28 C. Leung, *Passive Seasonally Responsive Thermal Actuators for Dynamic Building Envelopes,* University College London, 2014, p 197.
29 Kenneth Lawrence Bayliss, 'A temperature actuable opening arrangement with a wax-filled cylinder', UK Patent, Number GB 2466287(A), 2010.
30 Richard S. Levine, 'The Run Raven House', *Architecture and Urbanism,* 149 (2), 1983, pp 102–105.
31 'What can I expect from hempcrete in terms of its thermal performance?', *UK Hempcrete,* <https://www.ukhempcrete.com/hempcrete-buildings-thermal-performance-and-costs/>, 2014 (accessed 1 August 2020).
32 Suzanne Lee, 'Why "biofabrication" is the next industrial revolution', TEDSummit, Edinburgh, 21–25 July 2019.
33 Shigeru Ban, 'Emergency shelters made from paper', TEDx, Tokyo, May 2013.
34 Harriet Hawkes, 'Papier Mâché', *Building Conservation,* <https://www.buildingconservation.com/articles/papiermache/papiermache.htm>, 2019, (accessed 1 August 2020).
35 Doris Sung, Research Goals, DO|SU Studio Architecture, <https://www.dosu-arch.com/>, 2020 (accessed 27 March 2020).
36 InVert™ window shading system, TBM Designs LLC, <https://www.tbm-designs.com/>, 2020 (accessed 28 March 2020).
37 Mariam Bowley, *The British Building Industry,* Cambridge University Press, 1966, p 76.
38 Erich Schneider, 'Schumpeter's Early German Work 1906–1917', in S.E. Harris (ed.), *Schumpeter: Social Scientist,* Harvard University Press, 1951, pp 54–58.
39 Beverly Russell, Eva Maddox and Farooq Ameen, *Fifty Under Fifty: Innovators of the 21st Century,* The Images Publishing Group, Victoria, Australia, 2015, p 23.
40 Alireza Javadian, *Composite Bamboo and its Application as Reinforcement in Structural Concrete,* THE Zurich, 2017, p 392.
41 Oscar Hidalgo López, *Manual de construcción con bambú,* Estudios Técnicos Colombianos, 1981.
42 'Architects are using drones to spray insulation materials directly onto buildings', Mashable, <https://mashable.com/video/drones-in-construction-spraying-concrete-like-materials/?europe=true> (accessed 27 March 2020).
43 Morris Cotgrave Betts and Thomas Arlington Huntington Miller, 'Rammed Earth Walls for Buildings', *Farmers' Bulletin,* 1500, May 1937, pp 1–25.
44 Dante Bini, 'A Pneumatic Technique for the Construction of Thin Shells', pp. 52–55 in D. Feder (ed.), International Association for Shell Structures (IASS), *Proceedings from the 1st IASS International Colloquium on Pneumatic Structures,* Stuttgart, 11–12 May 1967, p 52.
45 Will McLean and Graham Stevens 'Atmospheric Industries', in *AA Files: Annals of the Architectural Association School of Architecture,* London Architectural Association, 2015, p 40.
46 Graham Stevens, 'Desert Cloud and other works', School of Architecture and Cities, University of Westminster, London, 10 October 2013.
47 Martin Bechthold, *Innovative Surface Structures,* Technologies and Applications, Taylor & Francis, Oxford, 2008, p 9.
48 Cor-ten® (or weathering) steel is a high-strength, low-alloy steel that protects itself from corrosion by forming a protective oxide (rusty) patina. Cor-ten® was developed in the US in the 1930s and is a trade name for weathering steel.
49 Will McLean (ed.), *Quik Build: Adam Kalkin's ABC of Container Architecture,* Bibliotheque McLean, London, 2008, p 6.
50 Richard Buckminster Fuller, *Critical Path,* St. Martin's Press, New York City, 1981, p 209.
51 Donald E. Ingber, 'The Architecture of Life', *Scientific America,* January 1998, pp 48–57.
52 Jarred Mihalik, Melody Tan and Sekai Zengeza, *Evolution of German Shells: Efficiency in Form,* <http://shells.princeton.edu/Mann2.html> (accessed 20 March 2020).
53 Andrew Waugh on CLT, *Material Matters with Grant Gibson,* podcast, 2020.
54 Richard Buckminster Fuller, 'The View from the Year 2000', *Life,* 26 February, 1971, p 51.

55 'Healing Earth: A Diversity of Solutions', interview with Dr John Todd, Sustainable World Radio, 7 October 2019.
56 Ibid.
57 Ibid.
58 Akira Fujishima, Tata N. Rao and Donald A. Tryk, 'Titanium dioxide photocatalysis', *Journal of Photochemistry and Photobiology C: Photochemistry Reviews*, 1(1), 2000, p 4, ISSN 1389-5567, https://doi.org/10.1016/S1389-5567(00)00002-2.
59 Allison Dring, 'Ornament & Climate', TEDx Berlin: City 2.0, 2013.
60 Nick Parker, 'Building "eats" smog', CNN World, 22 July 2013.
61 Rosa Schiano-Phan, 'The development of passive downdraught evaporative cooling systems using porous ceramic evaporators and their application in residential buildings' in *Plea2004 – The 21st Conference on Passive and Low Energy Architecture*, Eindhoven, 19–22 September 2004.
62 'Bunhill 2 District Heating Network – Heating up London', <https://uk.ramboll.com/projects/ruk/heating-up-london>, 2020, (accessed 27 March 2020).
63 L. Rybach and B. Sanner, 'Ground-source heat pump systems: the European experience', *Geo-Heat Center Bulletin*, 21, 2000, pp 16–26.
64 Jon Henley, 'Rjukan sun: the Norwegian town that does it with mirrors', *The Guardian*, <https://www.theguardian.com/world/2013/nov/06/rjukan-sun-norway-town-mirrors>, 2013 (accessed 7 July 2020).
65 'Steve Baer and Holly Baer: Dome Home Enthusiasts', *The Mother Earth News*, July/August 1973.
66 Atelier Ten director Paul Stoller with Laurence Dragomir, *Urban.com.au Podcast*, episode 42, 6 December 2018.
67 Harold R. Hay, 'Roofponds', in *Proceedings of the Eleventh Annual ASME Solar Energy Conference*, April 2–5, ed. A.H. Fanney, K.O. Lund, San Diego, 1989, p 140.
68 Daniel Overbey, 'The Invention of The Roofpond System', <http://danieloverbey.blogspot.com/2012/07/invention-of-roofpond-system.html> (accessed 6 January 2021).
69 Susan Roaf, *The Amazing Windcatchers of Yazd*, lecture synopsis, <http://www.payvand.com/news/20/feb/1012.html> (accessed 6 January 2021).
70 Ali Mahyari, *The Wind Catcher: A Passive Cooling Device for Hot Arid Climate*, University of Sydney, 1996, p 53.
71 Cedric Price, *Re: CP*, ed. by Hans-Ulrich Obrist, Birkhäuser, 2003, p 57.
72 L. Alfieri, et al., 'Multi-Model Projections of River Flood Risk in Europe under Global Warming', *Climate*, 2018, 6(6).
73 R. Barker and R. Coutts, *Aquatecture: Buildings Designed to Live and Work with Water*, RIBA Publishing, London, 2016.
74 Oliver Wilton and Matthew Barnett Howland, 'Cork Construction Kit', *The Journal of Architecture*, 2020, (25)2, p 138.
75 Ibid.
76 Richard Buckminster Fuller, *Nine Chains to the Moon: An Adventure Story of Thought*, Basel, 2019, p 270.
77 J. Krausse and C. Lichtenstein, *Your Private Sky, R. Buckminster Fuller: The Art of Design Science*, Lars Müller Publishers, 1999, p 212.
78 Alastair Gordon, 'War Shelters, Short-Lived Yet Living On', *The New York Times*, 31 December 2013, http://www.nytimes.com/2014/01/02/garden/war-shelters-short-lived-yet-living-on.html?_r=0> (accessed 3 February 2021).
79 Mick Pearce, 'Eastgate', <https://www.mickpearce.com/Eastgate.html> (accessed 25 June 2020).
80 Janine Benyus, 'Biomimcry Explained: A conversation with Janine Benyus', *Biomimcry Institute*, <https://biomimicry.net/the-buzz/news/biomimicry-explained-conversation-janine-benyus/> (accessed 25 June, 2020).
81 British Antarctic Survey, 'Halley VI Research Station', <https://www.bas.ac.uk/polar-operations/sites-and-facilities/facility/halley/> (accessed 3 February 2021).
82 Passive House Institute, <https://passivehouse.com/> (accessed 3 February 2021).
83 Gianni Botsford, 'House in a Garden and other projects', Technical Studies evening lecture series, School of Architecture and Cities, University of Westminster, 21 November 2019.
84 Ibid.
85 Eva Jiricna, 'Making Architecture', IE School of Architecture + Design, Segovia, <https://www.coursera.org/lecture/making-architecture/an-interview-with-eva-jiricna-AHFE2/> (accessed 12 January 2021).
86 HANNAH, Ashen House, <https://www.hannah-office.org/work/ashen> (accessed 13 January 2021).
87 Enric Ruiz-Geli, 'It's all about Particles', University of Westminster, 20 October 2016.
88 'Convention for the safeguarding of the intangible cultural heritage and its associated customs', 'Traditional craftsmanship of the Mongol Ger and its associated customs', Nomination file no. 00872, UNESCO, 2013, <https://ich.unesco.org/en/RL/traditional-craftsmanship-of-the-mongol-ger-and-its-associated-customs-00872> (accessed 8 July 2020).
89 Resource Library, National Geographic, 2017, <https://www.nationalgeographic.org/encyclopedia/yurt/> (accessed 8 July 2020).
90 'The UK Green Building Council (UKGBC) responds to Chancellor's plan to spend on energy efficiency in buildings', <https://www.ukgbc.org/news/ukgbc-responds-to-chancellors-plan-to-spend-on-energy-efficiency-in-buildings/> (accessed 13 July 2020).
91 NHBC Foundation, *Homes through the Decades, the Making of Modern Housing*, NHBC Foundation, 2015.

Index

Image Credits

Figs 1.01.1, 1.03.1, 1.03.2, 1.04.1, 1.04.2, 1.05.1, 1.06.1, 1.06,2, 2.00.1, 2.06.1, 2.07.1, 3.00.1, 3.08.1, 3.08.2, 3.08.3 and 5.03.1 Will McLean

Figs 1.02.1 and 3.09.1 RIBA Collections

Figs 1.02.2 and 1.02.3 Gianni Botsford Architects

Fig. 1.02.4 Sun Surveyor

Figs 1.02.5 and 4.04.2 Pete Silver

Figs 1.07.1, 3.03.1 and 3.03.2 Rammed Earth Consulting

Fig. 1.08.1 NASA

Figs 1.09.1 and 1.09.2 Rupert Heasman

Fig. 1.10. 1 John Farrell

Fig. 2.01.1 Made of Air

Fig. 2.02.1 Zbigniew Oksiuta

Figs 2.03.1 and 2.03.2 Heliogen

Fig. 2.04.1 From the Collections of The Henry Ford

Figs 2.04.2 and 2.04.3 Guy Sinclair, Fabrication Laboratory, University of Westminster

Figs 2.05.1, 2.05.2 Christopher Leung

Figs 2.06.2 and 2.06.3 Alex Sparrow / UK Hempcrete

Fig. 2.08.1 Biohm

Fig. 2.08.2 Photography Kris Graves

Fig. 2.08.3 The Living

Figs 2.09.1 and 2.09.2 Shigeru Ban Architects. Photography Steven Goodenough

Fig. 2.09.3 Photography Neal Lucas Hitch

Figs 2.09.4 and 2.09.5 i / thee and Roundhouse Platform

Figs 2.10.1, 2.10.2 and 2.10.3 Doris Sung, DOSU Studio Architecture

Fig. 3.01.1 Jan Balbaligo

Figs 3.01.2, 3.01.3, 3.01.4, 3.01.5 and 3.01.6 Ivan Davila

Figs 3.02.1 and 3.02.2 Studio Naaro

Figs 3.04.1, 3.04.2 and 3.04.3 Dante Bini / Binisystems

Figs 3.05.1 Graham Stevens Still from the film 'Desert Cloud' [1974].
Permanent Collection George Pompidou Center, Paris.
Photograph and copyright 1974 G A Stevens

Fig. 3.05.2 Graham Stevens Still of 'Wavetube' [1971] from the film 'Atmosfields' [1968-71].
Permanent Collection George Pompidou Center, Paris. Photograph Andrew Tweedie. Copyright 1974 G A Stevens

Fig. 3.05.3 Graham Stevens Still of 'Pontube' [1970] for 'Locations Edinburgh' [1971].
Permanent Collection George Pompidou Center, Paris. Photograph Andrew Tweedie. Copyright 1970 G A Stevens

Fig. 3.06.1 Jonathan Cole

Figs 3.06.2 and 3.06.3 AKT II

Figs 3.07.1 and 3.07.2 Adam Kalkin

Figs 3.07.3 and 3.07.4 Peter Aaron / Otto

Fig. 3.09.2 Oliver Perrott / RIBA Collections

Figs 3.10.1, 3.10.3 and 3.10.4 Waugh Thistleton Architects

Fig. 3.10.2 Waugh Thistleton Architects. Photography Tim Crocker

Figs 4.00.1 and 4.03.3 Emerging Objects

Fig. 4.01.1 John Todd Ecological Design Inc.

Figs 4.02.1, 4.02.2, 4.02,2 and 4.02.4 Elegant Embellishments. Photography Alejandro Cartagena

Figs 4.03.1 and 4.03.2 Rosa Schiano-Phan

Figs 4.04.1, 4.04.3 and 4.04.4 Islington Council

Fig. 4.04.5 London Underground Limited

Fig. 4.05.1 Skanska

Figs 4.06.1 and 4.06.2 Robert Bosch GmbH

Figs 4.07.1 and 4.07.2 National Archives, nos 412-DA-12868 and 412-DA-12854. Photographer Norton Boyd

Figs 4.08.1, 4.08.2 and 4.08.3 Atelier Ten

Fig. 4.09.1 John Maltby / RIBA Collections

Fig. 4.10.1 Bernard Cox / RIBA Collections

Figs 5.01.1 and 5.01.2 BACA Architects

Figs 5.02.1, 5.02.2 and 5.02.3 Matthew Barnett Howland, Oliver Wilton and Dido Milne

Fig. 5.03.2 Volgi archive / Alamy Stock Photo

Figs 5.04.1, 5.04.2, 5.04.3, 5.04.4 and 5.04.5 Mick Pearce Architects

Fig. 5.05.1 Photography James Morris

Fig. 5.05.2 Photography Sam Burrell

Fig. 5.05.3 Hugh Broughton Architects

Figs 5.06.1, 5.06.2 Gianni Botsford Architects. Photography Edmund Summer

Fig. 5.06.3 Gianni Botsford Architects

Figs 5.07.0 and 5.07.2 HANNAH. Photography Andy Chen

Figs 5.07.3 and 5.07.4 HANNAH

Figs 5.08.1 and 5.08.2 Shutterstock

Figs 5.09.1 and 5.09.2 Photography Urangua Sodnomjamts

Fig. 5.10.1 Scott Batty

Figs 5.10.2 and 5.10.3 Scott Batty. Photography Matt Chisnall

9781859469606